T
C
PE

es OF
WORLD
ERS

ACKNOWLEDGEMENTS

The author and Lion Television would like to acknowledge the contribution of the Time Commanders television production team and their research for the series, particularly Sophia Roberts, Adam Jessel and, most importantly, the series consultant, Dr Adrian Goldsworthy. In this volume we have made use of Dr Goldsworthy's contributions to the series detailing the background of battles, troop formations, weaponry and tactics. References to Dr Goldsworthy's works on ancient battles can be found in the bibliography at the end of this volume.

First published in Great Britain in 2004 by Virgin Books Ltd, Thames Wharf Studios, Rainville Road, London, W6 9HA

ISBN 0 7535 0928 8

Design and typeset by Smith & Gilmour, London
Printed and bound in Great Britain by Butler and Tanner Ltd.

contents

INTRODUCTION

Time Commanders: Great Battles of the Ancient World is an exploration of almost 1,800 years of military history which examines 16 battles that took place during a crucial period in Western culture. When Ramses II fought the Hittites at the battle of Qadesh in 1275 BC, Egypt was one of the great powers in the Middle East. It was a complex, rich society which was creating art and architecture that is still viewed as among the great achievements of human culture. When the Roman general Aetius surveyed Attila the Hun's hordes across the wide plain of Châlons in eastern France in AD 451, the Egypt of the Pharaohs was a distant memory. The Roman Empire was a fragmented wreck, with Rome itself about to suffer Attila's rapacious attack, and the Dark Ages were waiting to swallow the west in centuries of lawlessness.

The choice of which battles to include in *Great Battles of the Ancient World* was a difficult one. We have included Trebia and Cannae as examples of Hannibal's audacious assault on Rome in the Second Punic War, but why not the battles of Lake Trasimene and Zama? Equally, while Julius Caesar's military genius is represented by the battles of Bibracte and Pharsalia, it could be argued that the siege at Alesia or the battle of Thapsus were just as deserving of attention. We have decided, most importantly, to concentrate on land battles, and have also made it a primary consideration to pick out battles that were particularly significant for the warring parties. Leuctra, for example, saw the usurping of Sparta's military

dominance by Thebes, a crucial point in the development of classical Greece; Telamon was the last great battle between Rome and the Gauls in Cisalpine Gaul; Mons Graupius represented the most northerly point in Britain at which Roman troops engaged a very large number of British warriors. Our guiding principle was also to create as diverse and interesting a group of battles from the period as possible.

Preceding the accounts of the sixteen battles are a timeline and biographies of ten of the most notable historians to have provided us with records of the battles described in the book. The timeline covers the whole time period 1300 BC–AD 500, and relates the battles to the broad sweep of world history, allowing us to note, for example, that while the Greeks fought the Persians at Marathon, Iron-Age culture was spreading in West Africa and the philosopher Confucius was alive in China. The biographies of the historians are intended as thumbnail sketches of great figures such as the Greek historian Herodotus, but also as introductions to some lesser-known figures, such as Jordanes, the historian of the Goths. These biographies are useful in guiding readers towards the original sources of the information we have about the classical past, and to encourage them to consult such sources directly.

The accounts of the sixteen battles are treated as contextual discussions, not only saying who fought whom, but also describing the wider political and military events that contributed to the battles and the effects of the events after the fighting itself was over. Also included for each battle are more detailed descriptions of particular aspects of the conflicts, set apart from the main narrative text, and biographies of some of the most important individuals taking part. For example, a discussion of how soldiers in the third century BC could defend themselves against attack by elephants is included with the battle of Raphia, a battle in which Ptolemy, Alexander the Great's Seleucid successor, fielded elephants as a significant part of his army. We have also set out basic statistical information for each battle, giving numbers and types of troops on both sides.

Descriptions of the teams who took part in the studio reconstructions of the battles featured in BBC2's *Time Commanders* series follow the texts on the battles, plus a 'scorecard' of which teams lost and won their respective confrontations. These notes are intended as a record of those who made such important contributions to the television series, and as a testimony to the wide range of personal interests and working lives that can accommodate a passion for military tactics.

A bibliography and list of relevant websites follow. The bibliography is intended as a broad guide to the subject for readers of different ages and levels of knowledge. The list of websites is divided into sites on: general classical history; military history; Roman warfare and Greek warfare, and original sources. There are many sites available on all these topics, but we have tried to pick out those that have active links and are frequently updated.

Overall, it is hoped that the book provides a broad context within which some of the major military confrontations of the classical and immediately post-classical periods can be viewed and understood, and also analysed by war-gamers and tacticians of every stripe. It is also hoped that readers can gain a clearer knowledge of how we know what we know about such distant events and how, at times, we can be brought vividly into the thick of a battle by the turn of phrase of someone who died centuries ago.

TIMELINE

The purpose of this timeline is, above all, to place in a rapidly accessible, chronological sequence the sixteen battles featured in *Great Battles of the Ancient World*. The secondary purpose is to place those events in a broader, worldwide context that allows readers to appreciate how the rise and fall of cultures in one part of the world at a particular time are strands in a much wider story of humanity's development. The sixteen battles featured in *Great Battles of the Ancient World* occur over a period of almost 1,800 years, almost as long as our own era. During that time, huge changes took place all over the world.

We may be aware, for example, of the rough sequence of events in the Greek and Roman world, from the battle of Marathon to Julius Caesar's murder, but it is sobering to reflect that, while Hannibal was terrifying the citizens of Rome, the Chinese had begun construction of the Great Wall. It is also fascinating to observe that in the 1,800-year period under

discussion, almost all of the great religious figures of our own era were born: Confucius; Lao-tzu; Buddha and Jesus Christ.

Some battles in the sequence of *Great Battles of the Ancient World* are centuries apart, such as Qadesh and Marathon, while others, such as the sequences from Leuctra to Cannae and Silarus River to Pharsalus, are separated by much shorter time periods. These differences in time reflect how urgent the pace of change was in the Mediterranean basin in the fourth and third centuries, and in the first century BC. Very powerful realignments in the power structures of the region were taking place. Greek power spread abroad through Alexander the Great's astonishing career, but Rome's emergence as the world's greatest power spread its effects across the Mediterranean and beyond. By the time of the battle of Châlons in AD 451, even that monumental structure had crumbled and an altogether new world was coming into being.

c1300 BC Books first begin to be made in China

1300 BC The oldest known shipwreck

c1300–1200 BC Period in which Moses was alive

1300–612 BC Assyrian Empire

1293–1291 BC Ramses I, 19th Dynasty of Egypt

1291–1278 BC Seti I, 19th Dynasty of Egypt

1279–1213 BC Ramses II, Pharaoh of Egypt

1275 BC Battle of Qadesh

1275–1240 BC Period of the Trojan War

1250 BC Under the direction of Moses, the Israelites leave Egypt for the 'promised land'

1200–300 BC The Olmec people rule southern Mexico and northern–central America

1111–255 BC Chou dynasty in China

c11–1000 BC In Britain Stonehenge Phase IV: the path across the henge ditch is extended into the fields and over the hill to the River Avon

1004 BC David becomes king of Israel

c1000 BC In India the Rig Veda, the first Vedic literature, is written

900–400 BC The Etruscan period of Italian prehistory

814 BC Carthage is founded by Phoenician traders

800–750 BC The Iliad is composed by Homer

c800 BC–AD 20 The Mayan city of Takalik Abaj is founded

753 BC Rome is founded

745–727 BC Tiglath–Pileser III, Assyrian king

705–681 BC Sennacherib, Assyrian king

c700 BC The White Horse of Uffington, England

c604–531 BC Lao-tzu (Laozi), Chinese philosopher

c600 BC The Etruscans, believed to be natives of Asia Minor, establish cities that stretch from northern to central Italy

587 BC King Nebuchadnezzar sacks Jerusalem

580–500 BC Period in which Pythagoras lived

563 BC Gautama Siddhartha Buddha, the founder of Buddhism, is born

551 BC Confucius (d.479 BC), K'ung Fu-tzu [K'ung Fu-tse], Chinese philosopher, is born

550 BC The Persian Empire begins

529 BC Cyrus the Persian dies, leaving behind the largest empire to date; his son, Cambyses, succeeds him

520 BC Darius the Great rules over Persia

509 BC Romans overthrow their monarchy and establish a republic

500 BC–AD 20 The Nok people live in the area of present day Nigeria and use iron tools

490 BC Battle of Marathon

484–430 BC Period of Herodotus

c483 BC Gautama Siddhartha Buddha dies

480 BC 9 August, the Persian army defeat Leonidas and his Spartan army at the battle of Thermopylae

480 BC 20 October, Greeks defeat the Persians in a naval battle at Salamis

447–432 BC The Parthenon is built in Athens

431–404 BC The Peloponnesian war between Athens and Sparta

427 BC 21 May, Plato, Greek philosopher, is born

400 BC In India Panini's Sutra, the earliest Sanskrit grammar, is written

400–300 BC The Chinese suffer fierce attacks by nomadic herdsmen, the Hsiung-nu, from the north and west, and begin to build, for their protection, parts of what will later come to be called the Great Wall

400 BC–AD 250 Mongoloid people from Korea enter Japan and mix with the older Jomon populations

390 BC Gallic army sacks Rome

371 BC The ruling class of Sparta is decisively defeated in the Battle of Leuctra by the Thebans under Epaminondas

359–336 BC Philip II rules the Kingdom of Macedonia

355[356] BC Birth of Alexander the Great

350 BC First evidence of humans in southwest Colorado

350–338 BC In China Shang Yang rules the Ch'in Dynasty

336 BC Alexander inherits the throne of Macedonia and all of Greece

333 BC Alexander first confronts Darius, king of Persia, and defeats him at the battle of Issus

331 BC 1 October, Alexander the Great decisively shatters King Darius III's Persian army at Gaugamela

327–326 BC Alexander the Great passes through the Indus Valley and installs Greek officials in the area

323 BC Alexander dies in Persia at Babylon at the age of 32

322 BC Athens is brought under the control of the Macedonian empire

301 BC The generals of Alexander fight the Battle of Ipsus in Phrygia

c300 BC Iron-working has spread all along the savannah belt of West Africa

295 BC The Battle of Sentinum: Etruria is defeated by Rome and the Etruscan decline continues for more than 200 years

273–232 BC Ashoka, the grandson of Chandragupta Maurya, rules India

264 BC First Punic War breaks out between Carthage and Rome

241 BC The Battle of Aegusa, in which the Roman fleet sinks 50 Carthaginian ships

229 BC Hamilcar Barca is killed in Spain

225 BC Battle of Telamon

222 BC Cleomenes III of Sparta is defeated at Sellasia

221–210 BC Qin Shi Huang the first emperor of China

221 BC Hasdrubal is assassinated

218 BC Hannibal captures the city of Saguntum in northern Spain; the Second Punic War begins

218 BC Hannibal crosses the Alps

218 BC Battle of Trebia

217 BC Battle of Raphia

216 BC Battle of Cannae

215 BC Hannibal makes a treaty with Philip V of Macedon

214 BC In China, completion of the Great Wall begins

213 BC Hannibal occupies Tarentum

211 BC Romans recover Capua from Hannibal's forces

207 BC Gnaeus and Publius Scipio are killed fighting the Carthaginians in Spain

207 BC Hannibal's brother, Hasdrubal, crosses the Alps with a relief force

203 BC Hannibal is recalled to Africa

202 BC The Han Dynasty is founded in China

202 BC Hannibal is defeated at the Battle of Zama

201 BC Carthage makes peace with Rome

c200 BC Trade between the Arabs and East Africans on the Indian Ocean is established

c200 BC In Mexico migrations begin toward the area north of Lake Texcoco, where the urban center of Teotihuacan develops

c196 BC In Egypt, the Rosetta Stone is inscribed

180 BC The state of Meroe in Nubia becomes a great cultural centre

168 BC In the Near East, Antiochus Epiphanes rules over Israel and tries to outlaw Judaism

156–141 BC In China, Han Ching-ti rules the Han Dynasty

146 BC Carthage is destroyed by Rome and the land sown with salt

130 BC The Huns push the Kushan and Scythian nomads west across the central Asian steppes

c119 BC The Huns invade China

104 BC Rome faces a slave rebellion in Sicily

c100 BC G. Julius Caesar is born

c100 BC The Bantu-speaking people begin expanding and moving through southeast Africa

100 BC–AD 100 The Mayan site of Palenque is settled by farmers

90 BC Outbreak of Social War (Rome against its Italian allies)

89 BC End of Social War

88 BC Sulla consul in Rome

80s BC Mithradates, ruler of Pontus in the north of Asia Minor, makes war on Rome and overruns much of Asia Minor and parts of Greece

87 BC Sulla besieges Mithradates' allies in Athens

87 BC Halley's comet is observed

78 BC Death of Sulla

74 BC Lucullus is consul

73 BC Rome faces a second slave uprising

72 BC Lucullus defeats Mithradates in Pontus

70 BC Battle of Silarus River

69 BC Lucullus invades Armenia

69 BC Battle of Tigranocerta

63 BC Caesar Augustus is born in Rome

63 BC The Romans conquer the Jews

59 BC Julius Caesar's first consulate

58 BC Battle of Bibracte

55 BC Roman forces under Julius Caesar invade Britain

54 BC Caesar's second expedition to Britain

52 BC Battle of Carrhae

49 BC Julius Caesar leads his army across the Rubicon, plunging Rome into civil war

48 BC 9 August, Julius Caesar defeats Pompey at Pharsalus

48 BC On landing in Egypt, Pompey is murdered on the orders of King Ptolemy of Egypt

47 BC Julius Caesar adopts a modified form of the Egyptian calendar

46 BC The Numidians, a tribe in the eastern region of what is now Algeria, are conquered by Rome

45 BC The Julian calendar takes effect

44 BC Julius Caesar is murdered by Brutus, Cassius and other conspirators on the Ides of March

43 BC 27 November, Octavian, Mark Antony and Lepidus form the first triumvirate of Rome

42 BC Battle of Philippi

37 BC King Herod (d.4 BC) reigns over Judea

37 BC–AD 448 The Koguryo kingdom rules North Korea and part of South Korea, and the northeastern Chinese region of Manchuria

31 BC Naval battle of Actium in the Ionian Sea

30 BC Mark Antony commits suicide

30 BC Rome gains control over Egypt; the wheat fields there become one of Rome's main sources of food. Antony and Cleopatra commit suicide

27 BC–AD 14 Octavian, adopted son of Julius Caesar, rules as Rome's first emperor, taking the name of Augustus

c4 BC The Second Temple in Jerusalem is rebuilt

AD 1 The birth of Christ

cAD 1 Stone forts are built on the Aran islands off the west coast of Ireland

cAD 1 Settlers begin arriving in Madagascar from Polynesia

AD 9 In China the former Han dynasty ends

AD 14 Augustus dies and rule passes to Tiberius

AD 27–37 Tiberius moves to the isle of Capri, never to return to Rome

AD 33 Christ is crucified

AD 37 Tiberius dies

AD 37 The Roman Senate annuls Tiberius' will and proclaims Caligula emperor

AD 41 Shortly after declaring himself a god, Caligula is assassinated by two Praetorian tribunes

AD 43 The Romans conquer Britain under the emperor Claudius

AD 47 The library at Alexandria in Egypt is ravaged by fire

AD **54** Claudius dies after being poisoned with mushrooms by his wife Agrippina

AD **61** Battle of Watling Street and defeat of Boudicca

AD **65** Jews revolt against Rome, capturing the fortress of Antonia in Jerusalem

AD **66–73** Roman general Vespasian's army assaults the forces of Jewish rebel Joseph ben Matthias at Jotapata in Galilee

AD **68** Nero commits suicide

AD **69** Roman emperor Galba adopts Marcus Piso Licinianus as Caesar

AD **69** Vespasian, a gruff-spoken general of humble origins, enters Rome and is adopted as emperor by the Senate

AD **70** The Temple of Jerusalem is burned after a nine-month Roman siege

AD **78** Julius Agricola becomes governor of Britain

AD **79** Pliny the Elder, Roman naturalist, witnesses the eruption of the long-dormant Mount Vesuvius and is overcome by the fumes as he tries to rescue refugees

AD **81** Vespasian dies

AD **81–96** The reign of Domitian

AD **83** Battle of Mons Graupius

AD **96** Domitian is murdered and succeeded by Nerva

AD **97** 27 October, Nerva dies and Trajan, the Spanish-born governor of lower Germany, becomes emperor

AD **98–117** The reign of Trajan

CAD **100** The first Chinese dictionary is compiled

CAD **100** Raban Gamliel in the first century is credited with arranging the Amidah, considered by many the most important prayer in the Jewish liturgy

CAD **100–700** A group of agricultural Indians (today called the Moche) inhabit the desert margin between the Andes and the Pacific in what is now Peru

AD **105** Ts'ai Lun, a Chinese government official, is credited with the discovery of paper

AD **117** 9 July, Hadrian, Rome's new emperor, makes his entry into the city

AD **120–130** Hadrian orders a great wall to be built in northern England along with a series of forts 'to separate the Romans from the barbarians'

AD **135** The Jews are dispersed by the Romans from Jerusalem and the city is renamed Aelia Capitolina

AD **138–161** The reign of Antoninus Pius

AD **150–200** The temple of Quetzalcoatl in Teotihuacan ('City of the Gods') is built near what later becomes Mexico City

AD **161** Marcus Aurelius becomes emperor on the death of Antoninus Pius

AD **166** Roman traders reach China

AD **180** Marcus Aurelius dies and is succeeded by Commodus

AD **192** Commodus is murdered

AD **193** Pertinax is assassinated

AD **193** Septimius Severus is crowned emperor of Rome

CAD **200** Barbarian invasions and civil wars begin in the Roman empire

CAD **200–1450** The Hohokam people live in the area of Tucson, Arizona

AD **211** Septimius Severus dies and is succeeded as Roman emperor by Caracalla

AD **217** Caracalla is murdered in his baths

AD **220** The Han Dynasty ends in China

AD **235** Marcus Aurelius Alexander, Syrian emperor of Rome, is murdered

AD **238** Maximinus ('The Thracian'), Roman emperor, is murdered

AD **250–600** Early classic period of the Maya

AD **253–260** Valerian rules over the Roman Empire.

AD **269** Diocletian is proclaimed emperor of Numeria in Asia Minor by his soldiers. He had been the commander of the emperor's bodyguard

AD 276 Florian, emperor of Rome, is murdered

AD 284 Diocletian becomes emperor of Rome

CAD 300 Tiridates III, king of Armenia, adopts Christianity as the religion of his kingdom, making Armenia the first Christian state

AD 300–645 Yamato Period of Japan

AD 300–700 Goths, Huns, Avars, Serbs, Croats and Bulgars successively invade the Balkans

AD 305 Diocletian abdicates: Constantius Chlorus becomes emperor in the west and Galerius in the east

AD 306–307 The reign of Flavius Severus, compassionate emperor of Rome

AD 312 Constantine the Great defeats Maxentius at the Milvian Bridge and is instantly converted to Christianity when he sees a cross in the sky with the inscription 'in hoc signo vincit' ('in this sign you shall conquer')

AD 313 Constantine meets with the eastern emperor at Milan, capital of the late Roman Empire; they agree on a policy of religious tolerance. The Edict of Milan legalizes Christianity but also allows Romans religious choice

AD 324 AD   Constantine chooses Byzantium as his new capital

AD 337 Constantine, emperor of Rome since 306, dies

AD 337 Constantine's three sons, already Caesars, each take the title of Augustus; Constantine II and Constans share the west while Constantinus II takes control of the east

AD 350 A new state with its capital at Axum in the Ethiopian mountains grows and controls the coast of Eritrea and the sea trade route to southern Arabia

AD 378 9 August, in the battle of Adrianople the Goths defeat the Roman army

AD 383 Gratianus, emperor of Rome since AD 367, is murdered

AD 388 Magnus Maximus, the Spanish Roman emperor in the west since 383, is executed

AD 392 Valentinian II, emperor of Rome since AD 375, is murdered

AD 400 Chinese develop rigid metal stirrups

CAD 400 People from the chiefdom of Dal Riata in northern Ireland cross the Irish Sea and settle along the Scottish coast of Argyll

AD 421 Flavius Constantine becomes emperor Constantine III of the western Roman Empire

AD 429 Roman Africa is invaded by the Vandals

AD 431 The Council of Ephesus

AD 435–808 In Mexico, Yaxchilan on the bank of the Usumacinta, is occupied

AD 439 Vandals take Carthage

AD 450 The Hun invasions of India begin

AD 451 Roman general Aetius defeats Attila the Hun at Châlons

AD 454 In Italy, Aetius, the supreme army commander, is murdered in Ravenna by Valentinian III, the emperor of the west

AD 455 Rome is sacked by the Vandals

AD 476 The western Roman Empire formally ends at Ravenna as the barbarian general Odoacer deposes the last of the Roman emperors, the boy Romulus Augustulus

AD 496 In China, the Shaolin Temple is built in the foothills of Mount Songshan in Henan province

CAD 500 The Manteno people inhabit northern Ecuador

HISTORIANS

ammianus marcellinus (c. ad 330–395)

Although he was one of the great Roman historians, Ammianus was a Greek. Born into a wealthy family in Antioch (now Antakya, in west-central Turkey), he joined the Roman army and served on the Eastern frontier and in Gaul. He also visited Egypt and Greece. Ammianus finally settled down in Rome in AD 378, and began to write the book for which he is famous, his *Rerum Gestarum Libri* (*The Chronicles of Events*). The book was written for Romans, in Latin.

Taking Tacitus as his model, Ammianus composed 31 books, covering the years AD 96–378 in the history of the Roman Empire. Only the last 18 books survive, covering

the events of AD 353–378. Because he had been a soldier, he understood military events and could recount them accurately, as in his description of the emperor Valens' behaviour at the battle of Adrianople. Ammianus was clearly interested in different peoples and their habits and customs, as is shown in his descriptions of the Huns who presented such problems to the Roman Empire in the fourth century AD. Ammianus could also give striking descriptions of unusual events he had witnessed, such as seeing a ship hurled two miles inland after a huge earthquake in Greece in AD 366.

arrian (c. ad 95–175)

Arrian was a governor of the Roman province of Cappadocia (now eastern Turkey) under the Roman emperor Hadrian (AD 117–138). He was a soldier who defeated an attempt by the Alans, a tribe that lived in what is now southeastern Russia, to invade Cappadocia in AD 134. Besides being a soldier and an important administrator in the Roman Empire, Arrian was a writer of history and geography.

He is best known for his *Anabasis*, an account of the life of Alexander the Great. Although Arrian lived over 300 years after Alexander died, we know that his history is

accurate because he based it on the writings of Ptolemy I, a friend of Alexander who fought alongside him and later became governor of Egypt. Once his life was more settled, Ptolemy wrote an excellent history of Alexander's life, drawing not only on personal experience but on Alexander's own journal. As a soldier Arrian was able to use the information contained in Ptolemy's writings intelligently, understanding the challenges Alexander faced and overcame. Because of his careful use of original sources, Arrian is an important example of the evolution of historical method.

cornelius nepos (100–25 bc)

Born in northern Italy, Cornelius Nepos moved to Rome as a young man and became a writer of history. His best-known book, *De Viris Illustribus* (*Of Famous Men*), written in sixteen volumes, told the stories of the lives of generals, historians, kings, poets and other famous people in Roman and Greek history.

Cornelius Nepos was one of the first writers to create what we now call biography: the story of the life of a particular individual. In ancient times, this was a new form of literature. Also new for Roman literature at the time was his choice of subjects, because he wrote about foreigners as well as Romans. Only 25 of his biographies survive. Most of his subjects are, in fact, Greeks rather than Romans, but he also wrote about Hannibal and Hannibal's father Hamilcar. It is from Cornelius Nepos that we know about Epaminondas, the leader of the Thebans at the

battle of Leuctra. Cornelius Nepos used the method of writing about his subjects in pairs, to contrast them with each other. He wrote in clear, simple Latin, which makes his work enjoyable to read.

DIODORUS SICULUS (FIRST CENTURY BC)

Diodorus was a Greek historian who lived at the time of Julius Caesar and the Roman emperor Augustus and wrote what he intended to be a World History, with the title *Bibliotheca historia*. He lived in Rome for a time, and also travelled in Egypt.

The *Bibliotheca historia* was an enormous undertaking, filling forty books. Diodorus claims that writing it took him thirty years and that in researching his subject matter he made frequent journeys that endangered his life. Although not all of Diodorus' book has survived, we know that it was divided into three parts. The first deals with myths and history up to the fall of Troy, the second ends with the death of Alexander the Great, and the third part continues up to Caesar's invasion of Gaul. Although Diodorus was not the most accurate of historians, his work is important because it provides information from sources that would otherwise not have survived into modern times. So his description of the life of Alexander the Great, for example, helps us to understand events such as the battle of Gaugamela more fully than we might otherwise do.

HERODOTUS (484–430 BC)

Herodotus is one of the most famous historians of classical times. He was a Greek who travelled very widely, visiting Italy, Egypt, the Near East and the area around the Black Sea. At that time, travelling such distances would have taken many years. Apart from the evidence of his own eyes, Herodotus could also draw on a wide range of written sources on the history of his time. His great book is his *History*, which tells the stories of the Persian Empire and its wars with the Greeks, with a great deal of additional material on Egypt and Greece itself.

Herodotus' *History* is not only a highly entertaining piece of writing but the first great work of history in Western culture. He covers a wide range of subjects – military history and events, politics, religion, customs and social history – but constantly emphasizes that he is talking about things he has seen himself. Herodotus' account of the battle of Marathon is all the more thrilling because it took place not long before he was born, and he places it in the context of the much wider story of the constant struggle for dominance between the Persians and the Greeks.

JORDANES (SIXTH CENTURY AD)

We do not know for certain, but it is generally assumed that Jordanes was a Goth who lived on the lower Danube, although modern scholars suggest he may have been a bishop of the Christian church living in Constantinople. Although not a Roman, he wrote history in Latin, and is valuable to us chiefly as our most important source on the lives of the Goths and Huns in the early centuries of the first millennium AD. Jordanes' major work is his *De origine actibusque Getarum* (*On the Origin and Deeds of the Getae*), completed in AD 551. Jordanes also wrote a history of Rome from its founding to the reign of the Byzantine emperor Justinian (AD 527–565).

It is only through Jordanes that we know the work of the sixth-century Roman politician and historian Magnus Aurelius Cassiodorus, who had written a massive 12-volume history of the Goths. In his writing on the Huns, Jordanes preserves some of the work of another historian whose writings are now lost, Priscus, a Greek who travelled among the Huns. Jordanes is particularly informative about the collapse of Attila the Hun's empire after his death in AD 453.

LIVY (64 BC–AD 17)

The Roman historian Titus Livius, better known as Livy, was born in the city of Patavium (modern Padua) in northern Italy. Along with Sallust and Tacitus, he is one of the three greatest Roman historians. Very little is known about Livy's personal life. He grew up in Patavium and was not educated in Greece, unlike many young Roman men from the wealthier levels of society. It is believed that he moved to Rome in c. 32 BC with the intention of writing its history; it was only in Rome that he could have found the records and information he needed.

Livy wrote his history on rolls of papyrus, one of the few flexible writing surfaces available to people in the ancient world. Papyrus was a surface made from the pith of the papyrus plant that was sliced, dried and then glued together to make sheets for writing on. Rolls of papyrus were made by gluing single sheets together, end to end.

Livy's history of Rome became very famous, even in his own lifetime. It described Rome from its very beginnings as a city and state, tracing its history up to Livy's own lifetime. The work filled 142 books (i.e. scrolls) and the huge task took his entire life. Among his subjects were the Second Punic War and Hannibal's invasion of Italy.

TITVS LIVIVS PATAVINVS CVIVS INVICTO CALAMO
INVICTA ROMANORVM FACTA SCRIPTA SVNT
ROMA M D L XXII

PLUTARCH (C. AD 50–120)

Plutarch was a Greek writer who grew up and lived most of his life in Chaeronea, in central Greece. He did travel, however, and is known to have lectured and taught in Rome. He is one of the most prolific writers of classical times, dealing not only with historical subjects (in his *Lives*) but also philosophy, rhetoric (the art of debate and public speaking), debates on topics such as 'Are water animals less intelligent than land animals?' and antiquarian subjects such as the history of religious antiquities.

Without Plutarch, we should not have the evidence we possess about battles such as Leuctra and Silarus River, because he describes them in his lives of Pelopidas and Spartacus respectively. Plutarch wrote his *Lives* in pairs, intending that each subject be contrasted with the other in their attitudes, behaviour and histories, in such a way that his readers would feel they were learning about human nature. The pairs of lives also contrasted famous Romans with famous Greeks, because it was one of Plutarch's stated aims to increase understanding between the two nations and cultures. One of Plutarch's many skills as a writer lay in his choice of anecdote. In his life of Alexander the Great, he describes how Alexander succeeded in taming Bucephalus, the great horse he rode for much of his life. The horse was considered too wild to ride, but Alexander noticed Bucephalus was afraid of his own shadow. Alexander turned the horse so that his shadow was out of his vision, leapt on his back, and so tamed him.

POLYBIUS   (200–118 BC)

Polybius was a Greek historian who was exiled to Rome and detained there without trial, after the Roman domination of Greece was established at the battle of Pydna in 168 BC. In Rome Polybius mixed with prominent Romans and travelled to Spain, crossing the Alps into Italy following the route taken by Hannibal. Polybius is best known for his *Histories*, which were divided into forty books. He started writing because he wanted to tell the story of the history of Roman power from the Second Punic War up to the battle of Pydna, a timespan of 53 years. His account of the battle of Telamon was included in Book II of the *Histories*, and that of the battle of Raphia in Book V.

   Polybius was unusual for his time in the detail of his research: he took the trouble to read written accounts of historical events and, where possible, to talk to people who had taken part in them. He was one of the founders of the idea of historical truth. Polybius himself observed one of the most momentous events in Roman history, the destruction of Carthage in 146 BC. His accounts of the battles of Telamon and Raphia would have been written not much more than fifty years after they had taken place, so it is quite possible that he met people who had been present.

TACITUS   (C. AD 56–120)

Cornelius Tacitus is one of the greatest Roman historians, best known for three works of history: the *Germania*, the *Historiae* (*Histories*) and the *Annals*. The first deals with the tribes of Germany as the Romans had encountered them; the second covers the history of the Roman Empire from AD 69–96; and the third describes the Empire from AD 16–68.

   Tacitus is considered a great historian because he was able to describe a great many important events and people without losing his focus on his subject. He gives us first-hand accounts of the individuals who took part in the great affairs of the Roman state, emperors and politicians alike, in great detail and with considerable insight. Tacitus is our most important source for the history of the Roman presence in Britain in the first century AD. He himself had a source at the heart of events, because he was married to the daughter of Julius Agricola, governor of Britain in AD 77–84. We owe much of our knowledge of the battle of Mons Graupius, for example, to Tacitus' *Life of Agricola*.

QADESH C. 1275 BC

BACKGROUND

Because of the Egyptian pharaoh Ramses II's tremendous conceit about his stand against great odds, Qadesh is the first battle in history that can reliably be reconstructed in any detail. After the battle, Ramses commissioned pictures and accounts of the campaign, making sure he told history what he wanted it to say. Both an official record and a long poem on the subject were carved on temple walls in Egypt and Nubia, and the poem also survives on papyrus. Ramses was leaving nothing to chance.

Nevertheless historians are not sure about the precise year in which the battle took place. It was fought in the fifth year of Ramses II's reign, and can therefore be placed between 1300 and 1275 BC. We have decided on 1275 BC as the most likely date.

REGIONAL POWERS

The second half of the second millennium BC saw the great powers of the Near East vying for supremacy in what is now Syria. This region was both a crossroads of trade and rich in natural resources. The city of Qadesh was the key to the Eleutheros Valley and the Syrian Plain. The pharaohs before Ramses struggled for dominance with the kingdom of Mitanni, the Indo-Iranian empire centred in northern Mesopotamia that flourished from about 1500 to about 1360 BC, and then with Mitanni's Anatolian successors, the Hittites.

During the New Kingdom period (1539–1075 BC), Egyptian foreign policy was based on the principle that the best way to preserve the security interests of Egypt was to maintain military power as far north as Syria.

A peace treaty had been concluded between Egypt, under the pharaoh Tuthmosis IV (1400–1390 BC), and the kingdom of Mitanni that defined the borders between the two kingdoms in central Syria and recognized Egypt's claim to Amurru, the strategic valley of the River Eleutheros and the city of Qadesh. It fixed the idea in Egyptian minds that this border marked the true extent of the Egyptian empire, and that they had a natural claim to that territory. To the Egyptians, the valley of the River Eleutheros was of essential strategic importance because it allowed them access to northern Syria, and thus to territory in which military threats to Egyptian power might gather. But in order to maintain this route, the city state of Qadesh, which dominated the western end of the valley and lay astride the main Egyptian invasion route into northern Syria, also had to be under Egyptian control.

In the first half of the 14th century, the Hittites overthrew the kingdom of Mitanni; the balance of power shifted and the peace treaty with Egypt fell apart. The 18th Dynasty saw Egyptian influence in Syria wane. But with the 19th Dynasty came a new policy: Egypt wanted Syria back.

EGYPT

Ramses II was crowned five years before the battle of Qadesh. He was in his mid-twenties, a young Pharaoh in the prime of his life, and ambitious to expand Egyptian power northwards to include central Syria. This would bring him into conflict with the Hittite empire to the north, Egypt's most powerful rival in that direction. Ramses' father Seti had campaigned in the area around Qadesh, but after initial successes the Hittites had recaptured several of his principal gains. The young Ramses' desire to recover the region inevitably was a reflection of his father's policy. Egypt was a military state and, as heir to the throne, Ramses was trained for war from an early age.

He spent the first few years of his reign preparing his army. He expanded Pi-Ramses, a city in northern Egypt from which he would launch his campaign. In the fourth year of his reign he ventured north with his armies and captured Amurru, now a client kingdom of the Hittites; then he travelled through Tyre and Byblos. He now had the capability to attack Qadesh from two directions: from the south through the Bekaa Valley, or from Amurru. Having laid the groundwork for his plans, Ramses returned to Egypt.

THE EGYPTIAN ARMY

The Egyptian army was composed of Egyptians and mercenaries from various allied states such as Nubia, Libya and Canaan. It was approximately 20,000 strong, and was divided equally into four field divisions: Re, Amun, Ptah and Set. The personnel for each corps was drawn from a specific temple or estate region in Egypt and named after the local god.

Warfare then generally consisted of besieging or defending walled towns and cities, and the Egyptian infantry were important because they were the only troops suited to that type of soldiering. The capture of towns is very prominent in propaganda. Egyptian infantry were probably reasonably disciplined. Reliefs and grave goods show soldiers marching in formation to the sound of trumpets. However, the chariots were the really prestigious part of the army: they were the main striking force and it was in a chariot that Ramses himself fought.

Many historians have argued that the role of the chariots in Egyptian warfare was to support the infantry, but it is now generally accepted that the reverse was true: the infantry were there to support the chariots. Constructing the chariots required skilled craftsmen and a good deal of time. The teams that drove them needed constant training to be effective. Chariots were built for speed, to advance and allow the archer on board to shoot with his composite bow and retire out of danger. They could effectively herd and massacre scattered troops in the same way that hunters dealt with animals. The Egyptian infantry acted in support, providing secure masses of personnel behind which the chariots could retire to rest and replenish their ammunition.

The Egyptian field divisions were self-contained organisations, which could be employed as a single unit or separately. These divisions were commanded by men whom Ramses could trust: important landowners with a personal stake in Ramses' success. Communications between field divisions were maintained by riders or chariots. Each division consisted of 4,000 infantry (archers and close-combat infantry) and 500 chariots (with two men on each chariot). The normal pattern of deployment placed the infantry in the centre of the battle formation and chariots at the flanks.

THE HITTITES

The Hittite Empire extended over what is now Turkey and Syria, parts of Lebanon and the fringes of Iraq. Its control of the border areas tended to vary over the years as the balance of power with states such as Assyria and Egypt changed. At the time of Ramses' advance on Qadesh, King Muwatallish was supreme commander of the Hittite army and took a prominent role in the fighting. Muwatallish's reign is poorly documented, but we do know he was a strong and able ruler.

The Hittite army consisted of Hittites and allies and vassals from 18 different states. Like all Late Bronze Age armies of the region, its chief elements were chariots and infantry. The size of the army depends on one's interpretation of the main Egyptian texts: there are alternative figures of 17,000 or 37,000 infantry. But it was certainly one of the largest armies ever assembled by the mighty Hittite Empire. It included many mercenary troops.

Very little is known about the Hittite infantry at Qadesh beyond the fact that they were mostly spearmen. They do not seem to have engaged in the battle and their primary role may have been protecting the baggage and equipment.

Many troops in the Hittite army fought without pay, in return for booty. This was to be an important factor in the battle and may explain why the Hittite chariots were drawn into premature combat.

As in the Egyptian army, the 3,500 Hittite chariots were an elite unit of high status and the army's principal offensive weapon. Most chariots carried a crew of three men: driver, spearman and shieldbearer. Perhaps 1,000 of them were allied chariots armed with archers. Hittite chariots were probably stronger than their Egyptian counterparts but heavier and slower. On the Egyptian reliefs commemorating the battle of Qadesh, virtually all the Hittite crews are shown using javelins and spears, suggesting a desire for closer combat. At short range it is quicker to throw a javelin than to fire an arrow, and at very close range the spear can be used to stab at the enemy.

THE BATTLEFIELD

It is now widely accepted that the battleground had been agreed upon in advance by the two sides, although the hypothesis is not based on specific evidence. In spite of this agreement, neither side did play fair: Ramses arrived early, while Muwatallish deliberately planned an ambush. If the Egyptians had performed a more thorough reconnaissance once they had reached the area, the battle might have taken a very different course.

Modern scholars have suggested that the site of Qadesh gave the Hittites the advantage: it was in territory then under Hittite control; they would have access to supplies from loyal vassals; it was a relatively short distance from the Hittite home base; and the city was both large enough to protect the army if they lost the battle and in a strongly fortified position, surrounded by the River Orontes. The Egyptians, in contrast, were about a thousand miles from home.

PRELUDE TO BATTLE

Throughout March and April 1275 BC the Egyptians gathered, at Pi-Ramses in northern Egypt, one of the largest armies they ever assembled. At the end of April the army left Egypt by the coast road to Gaza, and there Ramses divided his forces. Turning inland with most of his army, he travelled through Canaan, past the east side of Lake Galilee, then entered the Bekaa valley and reached Kumidi.

A smaller portion of the army, the *Ne'Arin* ('Young Men'), would play a decisive part in the battle. They moved north from Gaza along the coast road to Phoenicia with the purpose of ensuring the loyalty of the Phoenician coastal cities along their route; they then marched inland via the Eleutheros Valley in Amurru to Qadesh. An elite unit, personally loyal to Ramses II, they were instructed to approach Qadesh

from the north, surprising the Hittites, who would
have been unaware of their presence in the vicinity.
Historians have put forward theories about what kind
of troops made up this unit and what their numbers
were: they could have been Canaanites dressed and
armed as Egyptians; they may have been one of the
four field divisions of Ramses' army, or an extra force.

Exactly one month after leaving Egypt, Ramses
camped with his first division (Amun) on a mound
called the Kamu'at el-Harmel Ridge, south of Qadesh.
The valley lay ahead, and Qadesh city was visible.
The other three field divisions, Re, Ptah and Set, were
behind Amun along the line of march and separated
by about 6.5 miles each (one *iter*).

THE COURSE OF THE BATTLE

Ramses and the Amun division descended from the
ridge, crossed the Labwi forest and then the Orontes
River by the ford of Shabtuna. Two Shasu-bedouin,
thought to have been planted by the Hittites to
misinform Ramses, told Ramses that Muwatallish
and his army were nowhere near Qadesh but at
Aleppo, 120 miles north. Ramses, for reasons we
cannot explain, does not seem to have ordered
reconnaissance to verify that information.

He advanced, eager to get the advantage of arriving
at the battlefield first, and camped slightly north-west
of the city, unaware of the Hittite force on the far side
of Qadesh itself. Arriving first at a battlefield was a
considerable advantage at that time, because it gave

the chariot

The chariot first made its appearance in Mesopotamia in about 3000 BC. Monuments from the ancient cities of Ur and Tutub show heavy vehicles with solid wheels in battle parades. On the earliest chariots the wheels turned on a fixed axle joined by a pole to the yoke of a pair of oxen. These Mesopotamian chariots carried both spearman and charioteer, although we do not know for certain whether they fought from the platform of the chariot itself or dismounted to use their weapons.

The two-wheeled form of the chariot was the one best suited to warfare. Such chariots were fast and manoeuvrable, qualities enhanced by the introduction of spoked wheels, which were much lighter and stronger than solid wheels, and by yoking the chariot to two, or sometimes four, onagers. The domestication of the horse in c. 2000 BC guaranteed the future of the chariot as a weapon of war. Faster, more responsive and with greater stamina than onagers, horses were the ideal propulsion power for chariots.

In Egypt, Anatolia, northern India and Greece, the use of chariots contributed significantly to the balance of military power in the ancient world in the second millennium BC. The manufacture of chariots in Egypt was established by 1435 BC; within 80 years light-framed chariots with four-spoked wheels were being used throughout the Middle East and had been introduced to Minoan Crete and the southern European mainland.

Archaeological remains from graves of the Shang dynasty (18th–12th century BC) suggest that chariots were being used on the Chinese steppes by the 14th century BC. Remains of chariots of c. 300 BC, found in a burial site near Peking, are similar in construction to Celtic chariots in western Europe. It is believed that the Etruscans may have passed the knowledge of chariot-building to the Celts, who were using chariots in Britain about the fifth century BC.

Ramses

Ramses II, also called Usermare Ramses, was the third king of the 19th dynasty of Egypt. His reign (c. 1279–1213 BC) was the second longest in Egyptian history. In addition to his wars with the Hittites and Libyans, we know him for his extensive temple-building and for the many huge statues of him found all over Egypt. Ramses' family came to power some decades after the reign of Akhenaton (Amenhotep IV, 1353–1336 BC). Ramses himself had experience of war and leadership from boyhood. He went with his father, Seti, on campaigns against the Hittites, and was given special status by his father as a regent, with his own harem and royal household. Ramses had the rank of captain in the Egyptian army when he was only 10 years old, though the rank may only have been ceremonial. Once he became pharaoh, Ramses continued his father's work in reclaiming territory lost during the reigns of earlier pharaohs. The battle for Qadesh was part of an 18-year struggle that Ramses waged against Hittite power. In 1258 BC the Hittites signed a peace treaty with Ramses which led to the development of friendly relations between the two nations and, in the years following, Ramses married one or possibly two Hittite princesses. Ramses also fought against Moab, Edom and Libya; it is principally upon his reputation as a soldier that his place in Egyptian history is based.

the army a chance to rest after a long march. The Egyptians were not, in fact, going to have this advantage: indeed, quite the opposite. The Re division crossed the Shabtuna ford on to the plain of Qadesh. Ramses' scouts now detected the Hittite force. The Hittites had sent out their own scouts to find out exactly where the Egyptians was. They were captured by Ramses, who discovered the deception and realized that the Hittite army were close by and ready for war. He immediately dispatched an order for the Re division to move quickly to the battlefield, whereupon it was ambushed by a force of Hittite chariots as it crossed the plain of Qadesh. The chariots crashed into the flank of the Re division, sweeping away the protective screen of Egyptian chariots. The number of the Hittite chariot force is disputed; in his account, Ramses implies it was 2,500, which would make it a detachment. With their chariot screen gone, Ramses' infantry companies lost their cohesion; unprepared for battle, they disintegrated in blind panic, the survivors fleeing northwards towards the Amun camp.

The Hittite chariots then turned towards the camp, raising clouds of dust, trampling the escaping Egyptian infantry or spearing them from behind. Panic overcame the Amun camp; defenders abandoned their positions and weapons as the Hittite chariots broke in from the western side. Many of the Hittites then slowed or stopped their advance, distracted by the lure of booty in the Egyptian camp.

Ramses was in his own camp, near the Amun camp. He put on his battle armour, mounted his chariot and prepared to engage the Hittite chariots single-handedly. Perhaps accompanied only by his small chariot-borne entourage, he attacked the Hittites on their eastern flank, wreaking havoc on a force whose cohesion and momentum were breaking down. Taking advantage of the speed and manoeuvrability of their chariots, the Egyptians began to pick off great numbers of Hittites. They attacked, turned, and attacked again at least six times. In the confusion Ramses was giving his troops a sense of direction by physically being in the thick of the fighting.

Muwatallish ordered a second wave of chariots to assist the first. There were probably no more than 1,000. Speed was of the essence because they had to get to the battle immediately to help the chariots that were reeling under the onslaught of Ramses' repeated attacks. The new Hittite chariot force headed for Ramses' camp rather than for his chariot force, to try to distract him from his attacks. At this point, the *Ne'arin* reached the battlefield, just in time for the Egyptians, and attacked the Hittites' second chariot force, joined by Ramses. The Hittite chariots were routed; a few escaped back across the river but most were killed. Many high-ranking Hittite and allied officers were killed, and many more were chased into Qadesh or back across the Orontes.

AFTERMATH

There are conflicting accounts of what followed. The Egyptian version, recorded in the reliefs commemorating the battle, relates that the fighting continued into a second day but, because he had suffered grave losses to his chariot force, Muwatallish offered a truce. Both armies then withdrew to their homelands. The Hittite version, based on material excavated from a site at Boghazköy, the Hittite capital near what is now Ankara, records that Ramses withdrew his army, in disarray after the events of the first day, and that Hittite forces then advanced to positions just short of Damascus.

What is indisputable is that Qadesh remained in Hittite hands and that Ramses suffered substantial losses to his forces. Some years later, Ramses signed a comprehensive peace treaty with Hattusilis, Muwatallish's successor to the Hittite throne. This treaty settled border disputes between the two nations, established a defensive alliance between Egypt and the Hittites and even included a form of extradition agreement.

MARATHON 490 BC

BACKGROUND

The Greek victory at Marathon had important implications for Western civilisation, as it put a hold on Persian expansion further west into Europe, which might have dramatically altered the course of world history. In the shorter term, the victory gave the Greeks an invincible belief in the value of their culture that would enable them to resist further attack and flourish into one of the most influential nations in history.

ATHENS

In 490 BC, Athens was one of several small, independent city-states on the Greek peninsula. The early Attic state of Athens was settled in the eighth century BC, and the first archontes (aristocratic chief officers of state) achieved their positions around the early seventh century. The earliest notable Athenian statesman was Draco, who during the 620s codified a series of laws whose severity is commemorated in the word 'draconian'. They were in operation for only a quarter of a century, when they were replaced in the 590s by the laws of Solon, who extended eligibility for political office and is often called the founder of Athenian democracy, though in fact his constitutional and political reforms were not comprehensive and did not endure. The young democracy was very active in the affairs of the Ionian Greek cities across the sea in Asia Minor. It competed for influence with Persia, which ultimately led to the battle of Marathon.

PERSIAN EMPIRE

The Persian Empire was the greatest power in Asia and southern Europe for almost two centuries, from 549 BC, when it was founded by Cyrus, until 334 BC, when its territories were conquered by Alexander the Great. It stretched from India to the Mediterranean and the western coast of Turkey. In the decades before the battle of Marathon, King Darius had secured the outer borders of the empire and pushed the eastern boundary as far as the Indus River.

DIVIDED LOYALTIES

The underlying cause of the conflict between Athens and Persia was the revolt of the Ionian Greek cities in western Asia Minor against Persian domination. The Ionian Greeks swore loyalty to the Persian Empire and provided it with troops but were not enthusiastic about Persian rule. Between 499 and 494 BC, the Ionian city-states rebelled against Persia and appealed to the Greek city-states for aid. Athens and Eretria responded and the major Persian city of Sardis in Asia Minor was burned by the Greeks. When Darius suppressed the Ionian revolt, he swore revenge on Athens. He also needed to secure this most troublesome of the empire's borders in the west.

In 492 BC Darius sent an army to subdue Thrace, in the process forcing the kingdom of Macedonia to swear loyalty. This put the Persians in a position to invade Greece from the north, but a storm wrecked their fleet, necessitating a second attempt. In 490 BC Darius sent a further 600 ships full of infantry and cavalry to subdue Athens and establish Persian might in Greece. Before the campaign started, he sent heralds throughout Greece demanding the surrender of all the city-states. In Athens there was pro-Persian sentiment in some quarters, following the deposition of the tyrant Hippias, who ruled Athens from 527 to 510 BC and then fled to Persia. The leader who replaced him, fearful of the Spartans who had deposed Hippias, toyed with the idea of courting Persian support to offset the danger from Spartan pressure. Although an agreement was reached with the Spartans, there remained a faction in Athens that covertly leaned towards Persia.

Darius sent Hippias in the ships to Greece under the command of the Medean Datis. Hippias was to agitate among the disaffected Athenians and provoke a rebellion, in return for which he would become governor of Greece within the Persian Empire. As the Persians sailed for Greece, the Greeks were in disarray: Athens was divided by political infighting and there was latent hostility to Sparta. Troops of the largest empire the world had ever known descended on a small group of city-states with no proven military record. The odds were all in the Persians' favour.

THE ATHENIAN ARMY

Athens relied for an army entirely on its citizens. The troops were called hoplites, meaning 'citizen soldiers'. It was the duty of every Athenian citizen to perform military service and to buy his own weapons and equipment. In that sense the Athenian army was not a professional force, but, unlike the Persian army, it was ethnically cohesive. Athenian troops were free men, which at Marathon would have worked to their advantage, because they were fighting for the preservation of that status.

The hoplites were divided into ten groups of equal size. Training began at the age of 18 and lasted for two years. The first year was concerned primarily with athletics, while the second was of a more intense and military nature. During the second year the hoplites were taught to fight as a unified army, with emphasis on group tactics rather than individual weaponry skills such as sword fighting. Extra tuition in the art of close fighting was given by private instructors for a fee, because the state could not afford it. An Athenian hoplite could be called up to fight abroad until the age of 50, or until 60 for campaigns at home.

The full military potential of Athens at this time is thought to have been 30,000 fighting men, but many of those would have been unavailable at Marathon and, even if they had been, would have been inadequately armed. For the battle the Athenians could call upon only 9,000 hoplites and 1,000 skirmishers. By custom, each hoplite would probably have been accompanied by a lightly armed slave who helped carry equipment and supplies and fought alongside his master if required. However, by the conventions of the day, these slaves or support troops were not counted by either side.

Traditionally the leader of the Athenian army was the polemarch, one of the three principal magistrates of the city. At the time of Marathon this office was held by Callimachus, who presided over ten generals, one of whom was Miltiades; each general headed a force from the ten tribes of the city-state. The polemarch was responsible for leading the army as it marched out of the city, and took the position of honour on the extreme right wing of the battle line. In terms of overall command, however, it is not entirely clear where he stood. Traditionally, the generals met as a board to take common strategic decisions, but it is possible that, contrary to the impression created by the Greek historian Herodotus (c. 484 430/420 BC), the polemarch retained overall command over this board. Herodotus, our chief source, may deliberately have sought to emphasize the role played by Miltiades rather than that of Callimachus. He tells us that five of the ten field commanders voted to have Miltiades as the battle commander, despite the convention of rotating days of command. If we believe his account, then, there was some continuity of command for the Athenians at Marathon.

ATHENIAN TACTICS

Hoplites did not fight individually but were members of the phalanx, a line of hoplites drawn up in ranks, who stabbed with their spears from behind a wall of shields. The shields were all-important: if they were discarded or lost, the phalanx could be easily broken. Because they were so reliant on their massed formation, hoplites could only fight efficiently on flat plains.

Unlike the Persians, the Athenians followed a policy of taking the offensive. The chief weapon of the hoplites was a long, heavy spear, and they protected themselves with their armour of helmet, shield and breastplate. Far more heavily armoured, and carrying pikes with greater range than the short spears and swords of the Persian foot soldier, the Greeks favoured close-combat battle formations, relying on their mass to break through the enemy line. They had no cavalry or archers.

Because the bulk of the Persian infantry consisted of archers, the Greek plan was to advance in formation until they reached the edge of the archers' range (roughly 200 yards), then continue marching twice as fast as usual in close ranks and bring their heavy infantry into play. They would therefore almost certainly end up fighting in disordered ranks, but that was preferable to giving the Persian archers more time to attack, even though the Greek armour was to some extent effective against their arrows.

Miltiades' battle formation was crucial to the Athenian victory at Marathon. The Greek centre was deliberately reduced from the normal eight ranks to possibly only four, in order to extend the line and prevent the Persian line from overlapping it. The wings, by contrast, were stronger, maintaining their eight ranks.

THE PLATAEANS

The small Boeotian city of Plataea, on the border of Attica, had been allied to Athens for three decades before Marathon. Plataea sought Athenian protection against Thebes, the most important city of the region, and its long-term policy of bringing the whole of Boeotia under its power. They therefore sent about 1,000 troops to help the Athenians at Marathon, where they were commanded by Arimnestos.

THE PERSIAN ARMY

We know much less about the Persian army than about the Greeks'. It was evidently much larger, but the sources enormously exaggerate the difference, some recording Persian numbers as great as 100,000. Eliminating the naval crews, logistic troops, attendants and camp followers, a credible estimate of the total Persian numbers may be 25,000.

As conquered lands were incorporated into a Persian Empire that stretched from the Indus to Greece, the Persian army became increasingly diverse. It included Sacians, Hyrcanian mountaineers, Khoassan steppe horses and Ethiopian archers, as well as Central Asian troops from the Oxus region, troops from the Euphrates region, Egyptian and Sudanese troops from the Nile region and Indian troops from the Indus region. The Persian army thus had no uniformity of language or fighting tradition, but at its core it depended on the original populations of the Empire, the Medes and the Persians, who were the best-trained and -equipped troops as well as the most highly motivated. The officers also came from these populations. It is most likely these were the crucial

MILTIADES

The Athenian general Miltiades was born around 550 BC, an aristocrat of the Philaid family, a prominent Athenian dynasty. He was appointed archon in 524/523 BC and later, around 516 BC, Hippias, the tyrant of Athens, sent him to succeed his uncle as ruler of the Thracian Chersonese, an Athenian dependency in the Gallipoli Peninsula. Relations with Hippias became strained and Miltiades was obliged to seek an accommodation with the Persians; hence he accompanied the Persian army on Darius' Scythian campaign. Yet he grew increasingly insecure and sought rapprochement with the new democratic government in Athens, cooperating with them during the Ionian revolt and helping to seize the island of Lemnos, possibly in 499 BC. When the revolt collapsed in 493 BC, he fled to Athens, where he survived a trial for tyranny and re-entered political life. His experience (he was aged about 60 at the time of Marathon) and ability made him a powerful figure, and he was elected to the board of generals to oppose the impending Persian invasion: a good choice because of his first-hand knowledge of the enemy.

Miltiades fought tenaciously at Marathon, though probably more to save his own skin than for any other reason. He had spent only a few years in the new democratic Athens and had no choice but to take up their cause. He claimed to have championed the breaking up of Darius' bridge of boats over the Danube, when he was on the Scythian campaign, but may have invented the story later to improve his standing at Athens. After Marathon he was given a fleet and in 489 BC made an unsuccessful attack on Paros. His enemies took advantage of the failure and had him fined. He died of a wound soon afterwards, but his son from his second marriage, Cimon, would become a major Greek statesman and general of the 470s and 460s.

TROOPS AT MARATHON

ATHENIAN ARMY TOTAL 11,000

9,000 Athenian hoplites, each armed with an eight-foot thrusting spear and a short sword and equipped with a *hoplon* shield, three feet in diameter, faced with bronze and highly decorated, as well as a *cuirass* (breastplate), usually of stiffened linen, but sometimes of bronze. The hoplite wore a helmet, usually of the Corinthian type, which covered the head except for eye-holes and was topped with a high horse-hair crest.

1,000 Plataean hoplites: Athenian allies, essentially identical to the Athenian hoplites.

1,000 skirmishers, most of whom were probably armed only with javelins. They wore virtually no protective armour and many did not even have shields. It was the custom to wrap the cloak around the left arm for basic protection.

PERSIAN ARMY – TOTAL 25,000

5,000 Persian archers, who wore a long-sleeved tunic, trousers and cap, were armed with composite bows and were inclined to fight in close formation, rather than as a loose line of skirmishers.

5,000 Persian *sparabara* (shield holders), who held rectangular wicker shields, from behind which the archers fired their arrows. Their clothing was similar to the archers'. They were also armed with six-foot long thrusting spears, which put them at a significant disadvantage when facing Greek hoplites in close combat.

2,000 elite Sakai bowmen, who wore broadly similar clothing to the Persian infantry, but a differently shaped cap.

2,000 elite Sakai spearmen, who carried short spears and (possibly round) wicker shields. They, too, wore largely similar clothing to the Persian infantry, but wore a differently shaped cap.

1,000 elite Persian infantry, armed with thrusting spears, swords and round shields. These held the centre of the line.

2,500 Persian infantry archers (skirmishers): these were the weakest part of the army, lacking armour or helmets, and so were especially reluctant to fight in close combat.

1,250 Persian infantry javelinmen (skirmishers): also a weak part of the army. Some might have shields, but none would have armour or helmets, and they disliked fighting hand to hand.

1,250 Persian infantry slingers (skirmishers): another weak element, some equipped with shields but none with armour or helmets, and undisposed to fighting hand to hand.

2,500 heavy cavalry, riding unarmoured horses. The riders may have worn linen cuirasses. They were armed with javelins, which were thrown before a charge, as well as swords or axes for hand-to-hand fighting. A few may have been equipped with longer *xyston*-style lances to match the enemy. However, the Persian cavalry presence at Marathon is disputed.

2,500 light cavalry, again chiefly armed with javelins and swords for back-up. These would not be armoured. There were perhaps some contingents of horse archers.

maraᴛhon and ᴛhe runners

The Battle of Marathon and the marathon race covering 26 miles are linked because the race is named after the battle. Legend has it that, immediately after the Greek victory, a fully armed hoplite ran the distance from Marathon to Athens, roughly 25 miles, to warn the people of the city that the defeated Persians, who had fled to their ships, might sail to Athens and attack it. Overcome by his exertions, the Greek soldier died after delivering his warning. The runner is often identified as Pheidippides, but Herodotus states that Pheidippides' run was in fact from Athens to Sparta and took place before the battle. The Athenian generals asked him, as a trained runner, to go to the Spartans and appeal for their help in the looming confrontation with the Persians. He is said to have travelled 150 miles in two days. In the event, the Spartans announced that they could not go into battle until the moon was full, five days after Pheidippides reached them, so the Athenians had to face the Persians without Spartan help. Nevertheless, the legend of the race to reach Athens lives on.

troops at Marathon, although it is uncertain exactly what ethnicities were represented.

Military service seems to have been compulsory for all Persians, nobility and bondsmen alike. Herodotus tells us that from five to 20 a boy was taught 'to ride and to use the bow'. The Greek historian Strabo implies that military service proper took place between 20 and 24, while Xenophon tells us that on leaving the army, Persian men remained subject to mobilization until they were 50.

PERSIAN TACTICS

The traditional fighting unit of the Persian infantry was the 'archer pair', consisting of an archer shooting from behind the cover of a large shield held by a partner. Such units would have been the crucial Persian troops at Marathon. They gathered in close formation so as to make a wall. Their key tactic was to wait until the enemy came close, when they would assault them with volleys of arrows from behind the wall. Thus the Persian fighting style was essentially defensive, despite the fact that they were the striking army at Marathon. They aimed to avoid intensive hand-to-hand combat; instead, being lightly armoured, they relied on mobility.

PRELUDE TO BATTLE

As soon as the Persian fleet sailed across the Aegean and attacked the city-state of Eretria, the Athenians correctly guessed the Persian strategy. Datis hoped to draw the Athenian military out of the city to march to the aid of Eretria, giving the Persian army the choice of destroying the Greek army in the open or bypassing it and sailing directly for Athens, attacking the city while the army was away. Hence, while part of the Persian army under Artaphernes was laying siege to Eretria, the remainder crossed with Datis and landed in the Bay of Marathon.

When Callimachus heard that the Persians had landed in the Bay of Marathon, he encamped his army at the shrine of Heracles, where he was joined by the Plataeans. A stand-off ensued for eight days as the armies peacefully confronted each other, the Athenians hoping to hold out until Spartan assistance arrived. However, on the ninth day the Athenians found out that Eretria had fallen by treachery; Artaphernes was now free to attack Athens. According to Herodotus, a huge debate followed between the Athenian generals about whether to attack, five voting in favour and five against. Begged to do so by Miltiades, Callimachus cast the deciding vote in favour. Despite the custom of rotating days of command, it was agreed that Miltiades should take charge. The battle line was drawn up. Callimachus led the right wing. Then came the Athenian tribes in order, while the Plataeans occupied the left wing. In order not to be outflanked by the Persians, the Athenians extended their line to make it of equal length to the enemy's.

TERRAIN

The Athenians were camped on the top of a hill to the west, while the Persians were camped down the hill on a plain to the east. To the south, and thus to the Persian left, lay the sea and the Bay of Marathon. Behind the Persian camp was a large marsh, flanked to the south by a beach where the Persian fleet was moored. To the north of the plain is the River Charadra, running roughly parallel to the coast.

THE COURSE OF THE BATTLE

In Herodotus' account of the battle, the Athenians began the attack. Their centre troops ran towards the Persians, who were astonished, thinking the manoeuvre suicidal, because they could see neither cavalry nor archers with the Athenian hoplites.

For the Athenians, however, this was the moment of psychological breakthrough. They had been intimidated for years by tales of how fearsome and invincible was the Persian army; now they were running towards them to fight and, if possible, defeat them.

Weighed down with shields, spears and armour, the Athenians built up tremendous momentum as they ran towards the Persians and, when they met them, struck with tremendous force, cutting deeply into the ranks. They fought furiously but were pushed back by the Persian centre. On the wings, however, the Greeks and Plataeans defeated the Persians; then the wings joined and smashed through the Persian centre. Routed, the Persians ran desperately for their ships to escape.

AFTERMATH

The Athenians secured seven Persian ships but the remainder managed to escape. Now the concern for the Athenians was that these, or the ships with Artaphernes, would reach Athens before them. However, as soon as Datis put to sea, the Athenian army marched back to the city and arrived in time to prevent the Persians from securing a landing. Seeing their opportunity lost, the Persians turned around and returned to Asia.

The victory was hugely significant for the Greeks, as it helped to give some solidarity to the disunited city-states. Ten years later the Persians again attacked Greece with an enormous force. They met defeat in the Battle of Salamis in 480 BC, and in two successive land battles the following year. These forays marked the last notable attempt to expand the Persian Empire. The defeat at Marathon did not in itself significantly affect the power of the Persian Empire, but it did give the Greeks the psychological advantage in the more decisive encounter ten years later.

LEUCTRA 371 BC

BACKGROUND

The battle of Leuctra was highly significant in the politics of ancient Greece, because the Theban victory ended the Spartan dominance of the Greek peninsula, entrenched since the Peloponnesian War between Athens and Sparta (431–404 BC). Sparta had had her day as the undisputed Greek power and would never again exert control over her rivals. The Theban victory ushered in a short period of Theban dominance in Greece, which lasted only until the death of the great Theban general Epaminondas in 362 BC.

THEBES

Thebes was originally a Mycenaean city, founded in the period of powerful Cretan influence in Greece, around the 14th century BC, and is rich in associations with Greek legend and religion; it was the birthplace of Heracles. Some time before 1000 BC it was settled by Boeotians and rapidly replaced Orchomenus as the region's leading city. At the end of the sixth century BC it began its struggle with Athens to maintain its position in Boeotia and Greece. In the Persian Wars, Thebes, motivated by hostility to Athens, sided with the Persians. When the Persians were defeated, Thebes was punished, and only the intervention of Sparta, which saw in the city a balance to the power of Athens, saved it from destruction. Thebes supported Sparta against Athens in the Peloponnesian War but, fearing Spartan territorial ambitions, withdrew this support and joined the confederation against Sparta in 394 BC. From then until Leuctra, it battled with Sparta for dominance of the Greek peninsula.

Thebes was one of the three main Greek powers, the root of its power lying in the Boeotian Confederacy, a confederation of the cities of Boeotia with Thebes at the head, enabling it to control the region. Thebes had first been head of this alliance in the sixth century BC, and preserving that status was a constant preoccupation of Theban statesmen. The King's Peace of 386 BC, which brought an end to the Spartan war with Persia, required the autonomy of all Greek cities and led to the dissolution of the confederacy, but Thebes reconstructed it under the leadership of Gorgidas and, above all, Epaminondas. Their fight to do so was the underlying cause of the battle of Leuctra.

SPARTA

Located in a fertile, mountain-walled valley, the city-state of Sparta was created by invading Dorian Greeks, who later conquered the countryside of Laconia and Messenia between 735 and 715 BC. In the seventh century it enjoyed a period of wealth and culture, the time of the poets Tyrtaeus and Alcman. After 600 BC, however, Sparta cultivated only the military arts and the city became an armed camp established, according to the official legend, by Lycurgus in reaction to a Messenian revolt. During the sixth century Sparta formed a confederacy of allies, the

Peloponnesian League. By dominating this league Sparta became master of most of the Peloponnesus. Although Sparta fought beside Athens in the Persian Wars, the rivalry of the two powers sharpened afterwards, coming to a head in the Peloponnesian War. Having won the war and wrecked the Athenian empire, Sparta concluded the King's Peace in 386 BC after a war with Persia and focused on entrenching its hegemony over Greece.

The Spartans were unique amongst the Greeks, a fact reflected in their constitution, which shared the rule of the state between two kings, drawn from two royal dynasties, so that one would check the power of the other. One king would command the army on campaign while the other ruled at home. At the time of Leuctra, the kings were Cleombrotus and Agesilaus respectively. Sparta was an intensely closed, conservative and regimented society. For two centuries it was the most feared fighting force in Greece. The Spartan legacy is not one of culture and civilization, like its neighbours to the north. The Spartans excelled at one thing: war.

POWER STRUGGLE

Plato claimed that the natural state of Greek affairs was war rather than peace. The constant jockeying for power between the Greek city-states is the central theme of ancient Greek history. The battle of Leuctra must be understood in this light and, more specifically, in the context of a wider struggle between Thebes and Sparta from 396 to 362 BC. After Athens surrendered in 404 BC and ended the nearly 30-year-long Peloponnesian War, Sparta was unquestionably the dominant Greek power. With Athens crushed, Thebes emerged as the most serious challenger to Spartan hegemony. However, a bloody trial of strength would leave both parties seriously weakened.

Sparta set about consolidating her political and military hegemony in all regions. The height of

Spartan power came in 380 BC when Olynthos capitulated and a Spartan garrison occupied Thebes. Occupation was particularly humiliating for the Thebans, because in 382 BC a pro-Spartan faction in Thebes had invited Spartan troops into the city, and that force took control of the Kadmeia, the Theban citadel. In 379–8 BC the Thebans managed to cast off this burden when some Theban exiles, including Pelopidas (who was to play a crucial role at Leuctra), liberated the city with Athenian help.

However, in the complex world of ancient Greek *realpolitik*, this Athenian–Theban alliance was simply a marriage of convenience to thwart Spartan hegemony. Soon Athens grew anxious at the rise of Theban power. Around 373 BC the Thebans reunified Boeotia under something like the terms of the traditional Boeotian Confederacy. Alarmed at such aggressive expansionism, Athens persuaded Thebes to attend a peace conference with Sparta. Athens and Sparta came to an agreement, but Epaminondas, perhaps eager for a confrontation with Sparta all along, refused to grant the Boeotian cities autonomy as the terms of the peace demanded. He insisted to Agesilaus, one of the two Spartan kings, that Thebes had never interfered in Laconia with Spartan business. After issuing a final ultimatum to Thebes, the Spartans sent their other king, Cleombrotus, who was on campaign in Phocis, to Boeotia with his army.

TACTICS

In antiquity the Thebans had a reputation for physical power and determination to fight hard in battle. Their infantry was grouped in deeper ranks than was usual among the Greeks at that time, when eight to twelve shields were the norm: at Leuctra the ranks were fifty deep. This exposed the troops' flanks more (at Leuctra they were eight shields wide) and the initial effect of spear thrusts was reduced as more men were taken out of the front ranks are moved to the rear. However, it did allow the troops to push deeper into the enemy, as all the shields made for more thrust. Brute force dominated the Thebans' approach: the hope was that the simple physical pushing power of the Boeotian army would penetrate the enemy's ranks and then break them before the enemy could destroy the Theban flanks.

Like all Greek phalanxes, the Thebans were looking for a balance of staying put and pushing power that would allow them maximum shield-thrusting and spear-penetration. The most experienced troops were in front and at the back: the less seasoned troops would stay in the middle and use their strength to push.

Epaminondas realized that smashing the Spartan troops on their right flank would destroy the morale of the entire Peloponnesian army and preempt the traditional Spartan tactic of rolling up opponents with a flanking movement from the right. He attacked diagonally from the side, instead of head-on, to exploit the fact that the enemy's shields were held on their left arms. He also used integrated cavalry tactics to ensure that the Boeotians could protect their ponderous and unwieldy infantry columns from light-armed enemy skirmishers.

Some historians, however, argue that his tactics at Leuctra were more utilitarian than revolutionary, as they were essentially adapted to the Theban national character and its limited strategic ambitions. They maintain that cavalry had been used in close concert with infantry on various occasions previously, for instance by the Syracusans on Sicily in 413 BC, as had deeper phalanx formations, for example at Nemea in 394 BC, and that the placing of elite troops on the left to knock out the enemy's right flank had been employed at Tegyra in 375 BC. Nevertheless, Epaminondas' tactics were perfect for the time and place: men fighting for land they owned against an attack by outsiders, led by a general they admired who enhanced their sense of liberty.

CLEOMBROTUS

Cleombrotus is not renowned as one of Sparta's great kings, perhaps largely because he was overshadowed by Agesilaus, his co-ruler. Cleombrotus came to the throne in 380 BC and ruled until 371 BC, when he died at Leuctra. True to Spartan ideals, he fought bravely at the battle. He seems to have had reservations about Agesilaus' aggressive policy towards Thebes but he led the army all the same, fearing the consequences of a political trial if he refused. Spartan generals were rarely easy opponents and Cleombrotus had plenty of experience, but he was clearly tactically outwitted by Epaminondas at Leuctra.

TRAINING SPARTAN WARRIORS

The reputation of the Spartan army was fearsome. By the time of the battle of Leuctra, the Spartan hoplite had been by far the most formidable soldier in the Greek world for two centuries. In close combat no one expected to defeat him. The Spartans were the only full-time professional army in ancient Greece: truly an elite force. More often than not, this army did not even have to engage, for the opposition would flee as the Spartan phalanx marched smoothly towards them. The institutions of the Spartan state and their system of education were organized with a view to creating superbly trained soldiers. Aristotle believed their constitution was so geared towards militarism that the Spartans did not know how to live in peace.

In Spartan society, such was the premium placed on prowess on the battlefield that a family might suffer more if one of their members survived a battle than if he died. Dying on the battlefield was the ultimate Spartan virtue. Leaving one's post in battle, however, was wholly unforgivable, and a man who did so, when he returned to Sparta, was forced to wear special clothes and to shave one side of his face; anyone who met him on the street was allowed to attack him, and it was illegal for him to fight back.

Military training started for a boy at the age of five, when he was taken away to a barracks. When he had reached the age of 12, he trained either naked or wearing only a thin cloak, in order to help him withstand extreme temperatures. He was fed on a minimal diet so that he would always be able to work on an empty stomach, and also because it was believed that it would make him grow tall and thin. He was allowed to supplement his diet by stealing, in order to increase his cunning, but if caught he was heavily punished, for being caught rather than for stealing.

The army was led the by the king, and under him the polemarchs, who were responsible for transmitting his commands to the troops through the officers in charge of units. The structure of the Spartan army is debated, but from what Xenophon tells us it may have been as follows: there were basic files of eight men; four files made an *enomotia* (platoon), commanded by an *enomotarch*; two *enomotiai* comprised a *pentekostys* (company), commanded by a *pentekonter*; two *pentekostys* made a *lochos* (battalion); and four *lochoi* comprised a *mora* (regiment of about 500 men), commanded by a polemarch.

The *enomotiai* marched one behind another in column. When deploying for battle, rear units formed up on the left of the leader, making a phalanx of four columns, 16 abreast and eight deep with two metres between columns. On the command to form close order, the rear half of each *enomotia* would move up to fill the gap on each file's left.

TACTICS

Perhaps the Spartans' most important intellectual contribution to warfare was the divisional concept: they pioneered separate groupings of troops, each capable of independent but coordinated operations.

By contrast to the more amateurish Thebans, who relied on brute force, the Spartans were extremely well trained and disciplined. Their phalanx (at Leuctra the customary 12 ranks deep) was capable of complicated reversals and flanking movements. Their most significant manoeuvre was wheeling their line round to face the left in order to roll up the enemy line by attacking it in the flank, a tactic devised when the Spartans began to fight wars with allies in the fifth century. The Spartans would always occupy the right flank and, after the inevitable defeat of the enemy left, employed this manoeuvre to deal with the remainder of the enemy army. They marched into battle to the sound of the flute (more like a modern oboe or bassoon), which was supposed to have a steadying effect that kept their ranks in very tight order.

TERRAIN

The Spartans were camped on low sloping hills to the north, while the Thebans were camped on similar terrain to the south. Between lay the battlefield, which was essentially flat, as it had to be for hoplite warfare. The battlefield formed part of the great plain of Boeotia, where numerous battles were fought. With its narrow entries and exits, it was the obvious collision point for hoplite armies descending from northern Greece and marching up from Attica or the Peloponnese. Ten major engagements were fought here over two centuries. Epaminondas labelled it 'the dancing floor of Greek war'.

PRELUDE TO BATTLE

Cleombrotus entered Boeotia over Mt Helicon to avoid the main Theban force which Epaminondas had amassed at Coronea. Having wiped out the small Theban detachment on guard, he advanced to Creusis, where he captured the fortifications and twelve Theban ships. Then, moving inland along the road to Thebes, he came to the plain of Leuctra and encamped on the hills to its north, while the Thebans and other Boeotians established themselves on the

epaminondas

A Theban to the core, Epaminondas (c. 410–362 BC) is remembered as a great tactician, general and statesman. Apart from Alexander the Great and perhaps Philip of Macedon, Alexander's father, he was possibly the most able of all Greek generals; certainly the Greeks venerated him as such. Thebes reached the zenith of its power under his leadership, only to decline after his death in 362 BC. A very severe man, he would not tolerate any kind of lie, even as a joke. As a young man he had trained himself in ascetic ways and had studied music and the philosophy of Pythagoras, preferring these pursuits to the company of his peers.

According to the Roman historian Cornelius Nepos (c. 100–c. 25 BC), Epaminondas was one of the greatest Greek statesmen and generals, developing new military tactics later perfected by Philip of Macedon and Alexander the Great. His abilities contributed enormously to ending Sparta's stranglehold over the rest of Greece.

The story is told that at the battle of Mantinea Epaminondas was severely injured by a spear-thrust. He knew that if he pulled the spear out of his side he would die, and chose not to do so until he was told that the Boeotians had won the battle. 'I have lived long enough,' he said, 'for I die unconquered.' The spearhead was taken out and he died straightaway.

Epaminondas never married. When reproached for not leaving any children to carry on his line, he replied, 'I will not lack a place in history, because I leave behind me a daughter, the victory of Leuctra, that will not merely survive me, but be immortal.'

slope at the opposite side of the plain. After debating
with the other Boeotian commanders about whether
they should fight, Epaminondas, backed by Pelopidas,
won his case and prepared his soldiers for combat.
Doubting the loyalty of some of the Boeotian allies,
he gave them permission to leave, but, says Xenophon,
they were misguidedly driven back to their camp by
overzealous Spartan mercenaries and some of their
allies, who had been drinking in the middle of the
day, as was their custom.

The larger Spartan force had taken their morning
meal, perhaps still expecting the Thebans to negotiate
or even withdraw. However, when it became apparent
this was not the case, Cleombrotus held his last
council. It was then that the Spartan army started
drinking, for according to Xenophon they thought
drinking in the middle of the day fanned their
aggression. So Cleombrotus drew up his now rather
drunk army, unusually placing his cavalry in front of
his infantry. The latter were in a long line, twelve ranks
deep in the classical Greek manner, with the best
warriors on the right wing. Epaminondas responded
with his now legendary tactical innovation, forming
his battle line in echelon with his right flank refused,
while on his left flank he advanced the Thebans in
a compact column fifty ranks deep, stiffened by the
300 of Pelopidas' Sacred Band. He too placed his
cavalry in front of his infantry.

THE COURSE OF THE BATTLE

Historians ancient and modern debate the precise
course of the battle. However, three facts stand
out, to which any reconstruction must attempt to
do justice.

The Theban infantry advanced diagonally towards
the Spartan line and, in response, Cleombrotus tried to
swing his right wing forwards to envelop the Thebans.

A cavalry skirmish took place just before the
infantry made contact, in which the inferior Spartans

were quickly defeated and fell back on the hoplites behind them, causing some disruption.

The Theban infantry encountered Cleombrotus unexpectedly quickly, partly because Pelopidas and the Sacred Band moved at speed from their station at the front left of the phalanx and fell on the Spartan right wing before it could complete its intended enveloping manoeuvre.

The shock of the impact as the Theban column and the Spartan line came together was considerable. With advantages in both mass and impetus (the Theban ranks were 50 deep, the Spartans' only 12), coupled with the fanatical bravery of the Sacred Band, the Theban pressure began to buckle the Spartan line. In the fierce hand-to-hand combat that ensued, many on the Spartan right wing perished, including, crucially, Cleombrotus, who died soon after being carried from the battlefield. Thereupon the Spartan flank gave way and retreated to the protection of their entrenched camp. The Spartan allies, who numerically made up the bulk of Cleombrotus' forces, happily followed. Like much of the Theban army, they had not engaged at all.

This reverse compelled the Spartans to admit defeat. Utterly dispirited, they declined an invitation to renew the battle and asked for a burial truce to remove their dead. Epaminondas then employed his final stratagem, granting the truce on condition that the bodies of the Spartan allies were buried before those of the Spartans. The extent of the Spartan losses (in the vicinity of 1,000) was thereby made obvious, to their great dismay.

DECISIVE FACTORS

The crux of Epaminondas' successful strategy was his deliberate concentration of attack on the vital point of the enemy line. Historians argue about precisely how he achieved this, but it is generally agreed that it was a remarkable tactical innovation. Refusing his right flank to strengthen his left, so that it could overcome the all-powerful Spartan right flank, contravened conventional military wisdom and practice.

The Theban elite force, the Sacred Band, which consisted of 150 pairs of homosexual lovers, fought with particular heroism and was crucial to the final outcome. On the other side, the implication from Xenophon is that the Spartans went into battle rather drunk. The battle took place soon after midday, at which time it was the custom of the Spartan army to drink, since 'it helped somewhat to excite them'.

AFTERMATH

Demoralized, the Spartans quickly returned to their city. Epaminondas did not take long to raise a great army – according to some sources 70,000 strong – and followed. He conducted a short siege without testing the defences of the hastily fortified Sparta, which by tradition had no walls and whose women, it was proudly said, had never seen the smoke of an enemy's campfire. The Spartans declined to give battle and, inexplicably, Epaminondas abandoned the siege. However, he did undermine Spartan hegemony in the Peloponnese, by liberating cities such as Messenia from their bondage.

Epaminondas then retired to Thebes, where he was charged and sentenced to death for having kept his high office for much longer than the month allowed him by Theban law. The sentence was soon revoked, after he gave one of his famous orations about his devotion to his mother city. For a time thereafter Thebes enjoyed its place as the ascendant power in Greece, although both Epaminondas and Pelopidas were killed at the battle of Mantinea in 362 BC, while fighting a coalition led by Athens and Sparta, who had combined against Thebes. Thereafter, Theban power rapidly declined. Sparta, however, had lost its dominant position forever. A manpower crisis was the root of the problem: Sparta was unused to such punishing defeats and, as Aristotle reflected, 'a single blow was too much for the city, ruined by its sparsity of population'.

TROOPS AT LEUCTRA

SPARTAN ARMY – TOTAL 11,000

2,000 Spartan hoplites, equipped with eight-foot spears and short swords, carrying *hoplon* shields three feet in diameter and wearing bronze helmets, probably the open *pilos* type which left the face uncovered. Most had linen or bronze cuirasses. They fought barefoot and their famous crimson cloaks were worn only when off duty or in peacetime, never in battle. These troops were superbly drilled and disciplined, as well as very confident.

7,000 Allied hoplites, equipped much like the Spartans but with more Corinthian and Attic helmets. These were significantly less effective troops than the Spartans. They would have come from Phocis, Acarnania, Corinth and a number of other states.

1,000 Spartan cavalry, equipped with javelins and swords, protected by helmets and cuirasses but without shields. These were troops of poor quality.

1,000 skirmishers, mostly armed with javelins, though in the battle a few of them may have been poor-quality archers. These were placed on the flanks to offer support to the main force but did not play a significant role in the battle.

THEBAN ARMY – TOTAL 9,300

The Sacred Band, a force of 300 crack soldiers, made up of 150 pairs of homosexual lovers. The Thebans, whose sexual attitudes were unusual even by Greek standards, believed a man would never abandon his lover in battle. Although they had a reputation as something of an elite, they were armed and equipped like any other hoplites. They were commanded by Pelopidas.

2,800 Theban hoplites, equipped with eight-foot spears and short swords and carrying *hoplon* shields three feet in diameter. Most had linen or bronze cuirasses and wore Corinthian helmets. Along with the Sacred Band, these were the crucial troops.

3,700 allied hoplites, largely similar to the Thebans in equipment. They were drawn largely from Boeotia and in terms of discipline and morale were inferior to the Thebans.

1,500 Theban cavalry, equipped with javelins and swords and protected by helmets and cuirasses but without shields. These were well-trained and of superior quality to their Spartan counterparts.

1,000 Theban skirmishers, mostly armed with javelins, though perhaps a few poor-quality archers would have been in their ranks. They were positioned on the right flank of the battle line, supposedly to offer protection, but did not play a decisive role in the battle.

GAUGAMELA 331 BC

Gaugamela was the decisive battle that brought Alexander the Great complete control of the Persian Empire. He subsequently gained its principal cities, Susa, Persepolis and Babylon. From that base, he would go on to cross the Hindu Kush and win military victories in India. During his short lifetime he would conquer more than half of the known world, creating perhaps the most significant legacy in history by spreading Hellenic language, trade, cities and art. Alexander is truly one of the figures who shaped the modern world.

He is also arguably the greatest general who ever lived, yet, although he is commonly hailed as a tactical genius, he is no less renowned for his extraordinary personal bravery and honour on the battlefield. There is a famous story in the *Anabasis*, the account of Alexander's life written by the Greek historian Arrian (c. AD 95–175), that neatly encapsulates Alexander's character. The day before Gaugamela, Alexander called a meeting of his commanders to discuss the plan of attack. The vastly more experienced Macedonian general Parmenio suggested an attack under cover of darkness as a strategy for overcoming the superior Persian numbers. Alexander replied, 'I do not steal victory.'

THE MACEDONIANS

Ancient Macedonia was part of what is now northern Greece. The Temenidae dynasty are thought to have ruled Macedonia from around 650 BC and established their first capital at Aegae. This dynasty claimed descent from Heracles and was related to the royal house of Argos in the Peloponnese. The Persians occupied Macedonia from 512 to 479 BC, but the Persian king Xerxes extended the area of rule for the Macedonian king Alexander I.

By its geographical position Macedonia formed a link between the Balkans and the Greek peninsula. Consequently, it had always had a difficult relationship with its more sophisticated southern neighbours, who tended to equate the kingdom with the uncivilized tribes of the Balkans. Language was a significant factor: the bizarre Macedonian dialect was frequently the butt of scorn from the 'cultured' south. The kingdom gradually became more stable during the classical era, despite intermittent dynastic struggles. It did not realize its full potential until Philip II took the throne in 359 BC. By defeating the northern barbarians and incorporating the Greek-speaking Upper Macedonians, he created a united, multi-ethnic kingdom. Most crucially, he centred this kingdom around a formidable army. Fourth-century Greece took a much more scientific approach to war, and Philip was at the forefront of this development, which enabled him to take control of the Greek peninsula.

His victory at the battle of Chaeronea in 338 BC, at which Alexander excelled himself, made Philip hegemon of the Greek League of states. When Philip was murdered in 336 BC at the wedding of his daughter, perhaps on the orders of Olympias, Alexander's jealous mother, he was succeeded by his precocious son Alexander. Within a year Alexander, aged only 20, had secured his position; he quickly eliminated his rivals and crushed rebellions in Illyria to the north and in Greece, the latter by razing the city of Thebes to the ground.

THE PERSIANS

The Persian Empire's origins can be traced back to early settlements on the Iranian plateau about 1500 BC. The first prominent leader of the Persians was the warrior chief Hakhamanish, or Achaemenes, who lived about 681 BC. The Persians were dominated by the Medes until the accession to the Persian throne in 550 BC of Cyrus the Great. He overthrew the Medean rulers, conquered the kingdom of Lydia in about 546 BC and that of Babylonia in 539 BC, and established the Persian Empire as the world's pre-eminent power. The zenith of that power was reached around the turn of the sixth and fifth centuries under Darius I, who ruled over a territory approximately encompassing parts of Iraq, Egypt, Syria, Pakistan, Jordan, Israel, Lebanon, Armenia, Central Asia, Caucasia and the Asian portion of Turkey.

The Greek view of this situation was that, ever since the unsuccessful Persian invasions of Greece in 490 and 480 BC, the Persian Empire had been in decline. However, we are overly reliant on the Greek perspective for our evidence. In fact the Persians continued to play a leading role in Greek affairs, as reflected in the various 'King's Peace' treaties. Nevertheless, in the decades immediately before the rise of Alexander, the Persian Empire does seem to have suffered a decline. It had to battle hard to win back control of Egypt, which it lost between 401 and

343 BC; it faced rebellions from some of its satraps (provincial governors); and from 338 to 336 BC it endured a succession crisis. Add to this the fact that the Persian army was greatly inferior to that of previous eras, and it becomes apparent that Alexander chose an opportune moment for invasion.

BACKGROUND

Philip's ultimate aim after unifying Greece under his leadership, albeit by force, was to lead an invasion of Asia that would exact vengeance on Persia for the invasion of Greece in 481–480 BC. His assassination meant this task was left to his son Alexander. Fiercely ambitious, the young king relished the prospect and, in 335 BC, landed in Asia Minor, intent on gaining the Persian Empire for himself. He landed with the most formidable army ever amassed on Greek soil, its nucleus the brilliantly disciplined and trained Macedonian soldiers he had inherited from his father. Nevertheless, few would have predicted much chance of success.

His motives for the expedition can to a large extent be explained by vanity. The throne of Asia with its unparalleled riches would bring him unprecedented glory. He could fulfil his father's wish and at the same time cast off Philip's shadow by outshining even his impressive achievements. Philip's cherished ideal of a pan-Hellenic crusade against the old eastern enemy, to bury the ghost of the Persian invasion once and for all, should not be ignored either: it was the most effective way for a Macedonian monarch to convince his sceptical neighbours of Macedonia's claims to Greek identity and hegemony. Insisting that the Greek cities of Asia Minor had to be liberated was effective propaganda. Besides these rational arguments, Alexander had more fanciful motives for the invasion: he insisted that he had a rightful claim to the Persian throne through his mother, and he was desperate to emulate his hero Achilles by waging a glorious Greek war in Asia.

By the autumn of 331 BC, after four years fighting in Asia, Alexander's achievements were already outstanding. He had conquered Caria, Lycia, Pamphylia, Phrygia, Gordium and Cicilia and won significant victories over Persia at the battles of Granicus and Issus. At the latter, Darius' royal family was captured and the king himself barely managed to escape alive. Furthermore, Persian military strength had been undermined by the loss of their best general, Memnon, in 334 BC. By 331 BC Darius had raised a new army, the nucleus of which was the substantial heavy cavalry of the eastern Iranian provinces. In 331 BC Alexander turned inland from Syria towards the empire's heartland in an attempt to capture it once and for all.

TERRAIN

The site of Gaugamela lies near what is now the city of Irbil in northern Iraq. The battlefield itself is a huge plain. The Macedonians and Persians lined up opposite each other, flanked on one side by hills and on the other by the River Tigris several miles away.

THE PERSIAN BATTLE PLAN

For Darius the large open plain of Gaugamela was the ideal place to meet Alexander's forces. Here, unlike at Issus, he would have the chance to make use of his superior numbers: his troops outnumbered Alexander's 5:1. His plan was relatively simple: he would spread out his battle line and outflank the Macedonians. The chariots, and a few elephants, at his front would charge, scattering the Macedonian phalanx and cavalry, so that his superior cavalry force could break through the gaps thus created, if they had not already enveloped the enemy. He set his engineers to work before the battle, instructing them to prepare three runways for the scythe-wheeled chariots. Furthermore, relying on his knowledge of Alexander's strategy at Issus, he knew how to deploy his units in

the battle line. With his scouts in place, he would know of Alexander's approach with plenty of time to spare.

THE STRUCTURE OF THE PERSIAN ARMY

It is very difficult to estimate the size and structure of the Persian army at Gaugamela. Some sources quote figures as high as 200,000 cavalry and 1,000,000 infantry. It is clear that Darius' army reflected the huge empire in its diversity. Consequently it was not a cohesive force, in stark contrast to Alexander's army. The Persian army was not the force of old, and Persian monarchs had come to rely increasingly on Greek mercenaries, as Darius had at the battle of Issus in southern Turkey in 333 BC. Following that disaster he made some attempt to change the composition of his army. Diodorus Siculus, a Greek historian of the first century BC, reports that new forces of infantry were raised in Babylonia and issued with new swords longer than those previously in use. However, the vast majority of new Persian troops were ill-trained and ill-equipped infantry, with no experience of disciplined fighting and probably poor morale. In reality Darius was relying on his heavy cavalry, and to a lesser extent on his elite infantry. His huge force was in general unstructured and ill-disciplined. To coordinate an army of that size was an extremely difficult task in itself, requiring a degree of generalship and training that Darius did not possess.

DARIUS

The traditional image of Darius is that of a coward. At both Gaugamela and Issus he fled at the first sign of danger. Yet his reign began with more promise. He restored the Nile as a Persian river, after acceding to the throne in 336 BC in very unstable circumstances. It is clear that he was no military genius and he was unlucky to lose his most able general, Memnon, early on. According to Arrian, Darius was feeble and incompetent in military matters and accepted any

Alexander is one of history's most fascinating and complex characters. So many myths have evolved around him that it is difficult to strip them away and discern a true picture. His upbringing does much to explain his character. His mother insisted throughout his childhood that he was the son of Zeus and one can only speculate about the psychological effect of this belief. He had a stormy relationship with his father, which at one point forced him into exile. However, Philip clearly had ambitions for his precocious son. The choice of the famous Greek philosopher Aristotle as Alexander's tutor was a sure sign that Philip wanted him to be educated and regarded as a true Greek.

Alexander's ability as a commander is not in doubt. He demonstrated it from an early age with his impressive performance at the battle of Chaeronea, when at the age of 17 he won the loyalty and favour of the Macedonian army. His rapport with his troops seems to have been incredible. His willingness to share their burden, not least in battle, was extraordinary. A famous anecdote of the Macedonian march over the Gedrosian desert in 325 BC is very telling. The march was gruelling and several men died from the lack of water, yet, when a small amount was found and offered to Alexander, he publicly refused to drink it, insisting he could not drink alone. This immediately inspired his men to keep going. As a tactician he was perhaps even better. What really distinguished his leadership over his army was his ability to establish secure bases and lines of communication. He failed only once in virtually ten consecutive years of campaigning, during which he conquered lands from Greece to India. Those in charge of logistics for Alexander's army can claim to be history's greatest unsung heroes.

Alexander's failings are all too apparent as well. He seems to have had the largest ego in history. As he conquered the Persian Empire, his fondness for its autocratic traditions increased. He began to insist on Persian forms of homage, which alienated his Macedonian kin. He became ever more paranoid, eliminating those whom he suspected. Yet perhaps his most shameful act was the murder of one of his most loyal soldiers, Cleitus, during a drunken argument. Cleitus is supposed to have questioned his achievements, as the Macedonian nobles sat around drinking one evening; his impertinence was rewarded with a spear through the neck. Alcohol would prove to be Alexander's own downfall: he died in 323 BC after attempting to down an enormous quantity of wine.

council that told him what he wanted to hear. But Arrian acknowledges that Darius was moderate and decent, as do other sources. This was a tradition among Persian monarchs, who understood that tolerance was a prerequisite for running such an ethnically diverse empire. Indeed, Quintus Curtius, a Roman historian of the first century AD, tells us that Darius felt responsible for the wellbeing of the troops under his command, even if they hailed from alien nations and practised customs not shared by his Persian courtiers.

Before Gaugamela, Darius is said to have made three peace offerings to Alexander. Only Diodorus Siculus presents an entirely different picture of Darius as a vibrant, courageous and intelligent leader. If Diodorus is correct, Darius was an energetic 'Great King' who could easily compare himself to his famous predecessors. Whatever our view of him, Darius seems to have been, above all, humanly prone to agitation and despair. His murder at the hands of one of his nobles, Bessus, after the defeat at Gaugamela was angrily avenged by Alexander, who did not believe his rival worthy of such betrayal.

PRELUDE TO BATTLE

In striking inland from Syria towards the empire's heartland, Alexander chose to take the Tigris route rather than head directly down the Euphrates towards Babylon. The Euphrates route was more direct but was less likely to provide grazing for the army's animals. Alexander crossed the Tigris before Darius' host could close the fords, passing the last natural barrier between himself and the Persians. Darius, informed of Alexander's movements by his scouts, had left Babylon, moved north via Arbela (modern Irbil) and encamped just beyond the river Boulemus. He planned to face Alexander on the nearby large open plain, where he instructed the ground to be prepared for his chariots. Alexander meanwhile, after resting

his army by the Tigris, marched to the edge of the plain, having learned of the Persian location from a captured group of 1,000 elite cavalry. Scouts were sent down to inspect the battlefield and their reports prompted Alexander's general Parmenio to suggest the night attack that Alexander so famously rejected. Ironically, Darius was expecting just such an attack and kept his army awake through the night, while the Macedonians slept.

Darius had drawn up his forces in a great line, over four miles in length. On his left wing were massed his best cavalry, the Scythian and Bactrian, apart from the Royal Guard, in case Alexander's elite cavalry were also concentrated there, as at Issus. On his far right, another mass of lighter cavalry, from Cappadocia, Syria, Media and Armenia, was likewise prepared to encircle the foe. In the centre, alongside him, Darius had his Greek mercenaries, the Persian Guard infantry, as well as the mass of assorted levy infantry. Some of the latter were also formed into a reserve line behind.

Alexander knew he would be outflanked on both wings and so adopted a formation somewhat like a hollow square, but moved in an echelon formation towards the Persian right wing, thus refusing his left flank. Parmenio was put in charge of the left wing, while Alexander retained overall control of the right, leading the Royal Squadron of cavalry himself. Light infantry were placed in front of each of these wings. The pikemen, under Craterus, and the hypaspists, under Nicanor, formed the centre between the wings. Assorted guarding units were placed on each flank, diagonally to the main force in order to face an attack from any angle. A reserve line of Greek hoplites was also placed behind the front line.

Given that Alexander was vastly outnumbered, Gaugamela is a prime illustration of his military genius and the remarkable effectiveness of his basic tactical principle. In theory this meant pinning down the enemy line by means of the formidable Macedonian

THE GREEK VIEW OF THE PERSIANS IN CLASSICAL TIMES

The famous Greek teacher Isocrates (436–338 BC) sums up the Greek view of Persia in classical times: 'It is not possible for people who are reared and governed as the Persians, either to have a part in any other form of virtue or to set up on the field of battle trophies of victory over their foes. For how could either an able general or a good soldier be produced amid such ways of life as theirs? Most of their population is a mob without discipline or experience of dangers, which has lost all its stamina for war and has been trained more effectively for servitude than are the slaves in our country.'

The Greeks thought of the Persians as a decadent, barbarous tyranny, but it is clear that this was a hopelessly biased opinion. From what little evidence we have, the Persian Empire seems to have been a relatively enlightened regime, which understood the virtues of tolerance and civility.

infantry phalanx, then delivering the crucial assault at a selected point with his own Companion cavalry. Above all, Alexander was able to coordinate his different troops to brilliant effect.

The battle was won at three critical points:

✝ Alexander broke through a gap in the Persian left centre with his Companion cavalry moments before he was outflanked;

✝ Parmenio, hugely outnumbered on the left flank, held firm and prevented the Persians from getting behind the enemy line;

✝ The few Persians that did break through the Macedonian line were neutralized by the reserve Greek hoplite phalanx at the rear. In any case Darius had fled before such breakthroughs, and indeed before his army was properly defeated.

THE COURSE OF THE BATTLE

The battle began in the early morning. Keeping far to the left of the area prepared for the Persian chariots, Alexander initially appeared to be entering Darius' trap, but at a signal the Macedonians suddenly changed direction and moved diagonally right, away from the prepared ground. Darius, in response, attempted to extend his left-hand side, but his forces were cumbersome because of their size and could not match the speed of the smaller, better organized Macedonians. Darius sent the cavalry on his left to stop the Macedonian advance, but the Greek mercenary cavalry under Menidas, part of the Macedonian right-flank guard, charged them as had been prearranged. Initially Menidas was driven back, but Alexander sent two more cavalry groups into the fray, the veteran Greek mercenaries and the Paeonians, and these started to push the Scythian and Bactrian cavalry back.

With the Macedonians still moving steadily to the right, Darius had to send in his chariots before it was too late. However, those to his left, charging towards Alexander, were eliminated by the javelin-men and archers stationed in front of the Macedonian ranks.

Similarly, when those in the centre of the field met the phalanx, they simply opened ranks, allowing the chariots through, then drove their pikes into the passing horses – another prearranged tactic. Finally, the horses pulling the chariots to Darius' right were frightened back by the clashing of weapon against shield, which Alexander had also ordered.

Darius then ordered a full advance, and the cavalry battle on Alexander's right began to intensify. Throwing all but his light cavalry into attack, Alexander continued towards the point where the Persian cavalry joined with Darius' main line. It was then that he ordered the light cavalry to charge at this 'hinge'. The hinge broke and Alexander personally led his own Companion cavalry into the gap at full gallop, striking along the flank of the Persian infantry line. They thrust back the Persian cavalrymen and aimed their lances at their enemies' faces, while the Macedonian phalanx presented a solid hedge of bristling pike-points. Darius, from his central position on his chariot, watched his left wing crumble and saw Alexander and his elite forces cutting a passage directly towards him. He fled, and the mass of Persian infantry needed little incentive to follow suit. As Alexander pressed hard, the slaughter began. From this point, whatever else happened, the battle was effectively won.

AFTERMATH

Alexander, with the Companion cavalry and Thessalian cavalry, then gave chase to the fleeing Persians, who suffered over 40,000 casualties with yet more captured. Meanwhile Parmenio took the other units to capture the spoils at the Persian camp. After two days, 70 miles and the loss of 500 horses, Alexander reached Arbela. Darius eluded him, escaping to Media, where he was later killed. At Arbela, in a lavish ceremony, Alexander was proclaimed King of Asia. He was 25.

MACEDONIAN ARMY – TOTAL 47,000 (40,000 INFANTRY AND 7,000 CAVALRY)

11,000 pikemen (Companion infantry), armed with 18-foot pikes (*sarissae*), held in both hands, and a short sword. Their armour consisted of a stiffened linen (or maybe occasionally bronze) cuirass, a bronze helmet, usually of the Phrygian type, and a round shield faced with bronze and strapped to the left arm, since the man did not have a hand free to hold it. Originally these had been divided into six units of 1,500 men (about 9,000 in total), but by Gaugamela the units may have been slightly larger to make a total of 11,000. They were Macedonian natives, both *pezhetairoi* (Foot-Companions) and *asthelairoi* (Townsmen-Companions), and formed the linchpin of Alexander's army. They were also known as phalangites, because they adopted the phalanx in battle, and when in this formation were typically at least eight men deep, although at Gaugamela this figure was increased to 16. The phalanx Alexander used was essentially Philip's creation; he pioneered its training and paid it as a professional infantry. Its novel mobility enabled it to be used for attack or defence.

3,000 hypaspists (Silver Shields), so named after the squire who carried the King's shield in to battle. Their armour and helmet would have been similar to the pikemen's; the helmet may have had a crest of feathers mounted on either side of the bowl. There were three units each of 1,000 men (*chiliarchiai*), tested, reliable and often middle-aged veterans, reputed for their endurance – many had served Alexander's father. In battle they were often used to provide a link between the slower centre and the faster cavalry wings; they were also used in 'special forces' roles such as night operations. For example, at the culmination of Alexander's siege of Tyre, the Hypaspists led the attack.

12,000 Greek hoplites, armed with an eight-foot thrusting spear held in one hand, which enabled them to use large, round, bronze-faced hoplon shields, attached to their arms by straps at the elbow and wrist. They also carried a short sword and wore a bronze helmet, which could have been drawn from a range of Attic, Phrygian, Boeotian and Corinthian types. Body armour was not always worn, but a reasonable proportion would have had a linen cuirass and a handful may have sported bronze armour. Helmets would normally have had a horse-hair crest and shields would have been brightly decorated. These men were Greek allies, who reluctantly served Alexander as commander of the Greek League, and mercenaries, but were probably not divided into fixed units. As traditional Greek infantry, they were trained to fight.

2,000 Companion cavalry (heavy cavalry), the elite of the army, aristocrats obliged to share danger with their king. They were armed with a long spear (*xyston*), maybe as much as 12 feet in length, which was thrust underarm. After the initial charge, it was broken or dropped, lest the reaction force unseat the rider, who then used a short slashing sword. They did not carry shields but wore a stiffened linen cuirass and a bronze helmet, often Boeotian style but sometimes Phrygian. They were divided into eight squadrons, of which the royal one – the squadron at the head of which Alexander fought – was probably stronger than the others and may have numbered about 300. The others mustered perhaps 240 men each. The Companions fought in a wedge, a triangular formation with the leader at the point, the apex directed at the enemy, which allowed easy movement to the right or left and proved extremely effective in scattering opposing cavalry. Although incapable of a direct attack on enemy heavy infantry, they could easily exploit gaps, making deadly flank or rear attacks. Their prominent role at Gaugamela was typical, because Alexander always tried to ensure that he was in the thick of the action.

3,800 heavy Greek cavalry, about 2,000 of whom would have been Thessalians. They were probably armed and equipped much like the Companions, although there is a theory that they used throwing spears rather than the longer *xyston*. A conquered people who had been 'assimilated' into the Macedonian Empire, they were rich enough to be able to afford the horses and armour necessary to form a heavy cavalry unit. The elite unit of 2,000 was formed of some of the richest nobles in Thessaly. They fought in close formation, preferring to use a rhomboid shape rather than the Companions' wedge. At Gaugamela, as in many other battles, they were placed on the left wing. The other 1,800 were mercenary and allied Greek cavalrymen, probably equipped much like the above, with the exception that they may well have used javelins rather than the thrusting *xyston*.

1,200 light cavalry, 600 of whom were probably *prodromoi*. These were armed with the long *xyston* spear, and their only defensive equipment was a bronze Phrygian helmet; they did not carry shields or wear armour. Divided into four units of 150, they were originally formed entirely of native Macedonians, but had begun to accept Greeks into their number at the time of Gaugamela. They were responsible for one of the key actions of the battle, breaking the hinge between the Persian left centre and left wing. The other 600 were assorted cavalrymen; some were Paionians from the fringes of Macedonia and others, perhaps two thirds of the number, Thracian. The Paionians had thrusting spears

and wore helmets, probably of a crested Attic type, while the Thracians probably carried javelins and round shields. Lacking armour, they were not effective in shock combat but fought in open order. Their role was to harass the unbroken enemy and pursue enemies in retreat.

1,000 archers, in two units of 500, composed of either native Macedonians or Cretan mercenaries. Naturally wearing no armour, they did carry swords but were not well suited to hand-to-hand combat.

4,500 javelinmen, the most notable of whom were the Agrianian javelineers, who were supposed to be some of Alexander's favourite units. They wore little, if any, armour. Typically they used both javelins and swords and carried a small, light, shield. They did not fight in any specific formation, but were rather used, like the light cavalry, to harass unbroken enemy forces or pursue those who were fleeing. Although lightly armed, they were often surprisingly effective in shock-combat situations, and they were ideally suited to their primary role at Gaugamela, counteracting the Persian chariots.

500 slingers, probably Greeks of various sorts, and perhaps also Thracian tribesmen. They were not suited to close combat but effective in counteracting Darius' chariots.

8,000 peltasts, either Thracian or Greek. These were essentially skirmishers armed with javelins but carried a larger shield than the other javelinmen (some of whom had no shields at all) and were more willing to fight in close combat. The Thracians would be dressed in their ethnic costume of patterned tunic, tall cap and boots. The Greeks dressed much like the hoplites, but with less armour.

PERSIAN ARMY – 240,000
(40,000 CAVALRY AND 200,000 INFANTRY)

1,000 Persian Guard infantry, armed with thrusting spears, swords and round shields. They were known as the apple-bearers because of an apple-shaped weight on their spear butts.

10,000 Greek mercenaries, essentially similar to the hoplites in the Macedonian army. However, these troops had been beaten in every action so far. Alexander had refused to accept their surrender at the battle of the Granicus and massacred them. Their morale would not have been high, but was still probably better than that of the majority of the Persian army.

41,000 Persian levy slingers, some perhaps with shields but none with armour or helmets. These troops would be of extremely low quality. As undrilled skirmishers, they would be especially reluctant to fight hand to hand. They were part of the levy infantry, which made up the mass of Darius' army.

48,000 archers, of whom perhaps around 7,000 would have been Carians and Mardians, who wore the standard Persian costume of long-sleeved tunic, trousers and cap. They were armed with composite bows. The other 41,000 were Persian levy archers, who did not have armour or helmets. They were essentially undrilled skirmishers of poor quality and reluctant to fight at close quarters. Like the slingers they formed part of the levy infantry.

100,000 Persian levy javelineers, some perhaps with shields but none with armour or helmets. Undrilled, most would have fought as skirmishers, though perhaps a few fought in mass formation. Again part of the levy infantry.

20,000 Persian heavy cavalry, of whom probably about 16,000 rode unarmoured horses, though they themselves may have worn linen cuirasses. They were armed with javelins, which were thrown before a charge, and swords or axes for hand-to-hand combat. A few may have been equipped with longer *xyston*-style lances to match the enemy, but these do not appear to have played a significant role in the battle. They were divided into various contingents including Bactrians, Persians and a range of other races. The other 4,000 were probably *cataphracts* (heavy cavalry), made up largely of more Bactrians, Massagetai, Cappadocians and Armenians, each group about 1,000 strong. The first two groups, and probably the second two as well, rode armoured horses and were probably also armoured themselves. They were probably equipped with javelins, which were thrown before combat, and swords. They do not appear to have had shields. These troops were Darius' prize possession, accomplished horsemen whose fearsome charge could exploit gaps in an enemy line and offer formidable opposition to enemy cavalry.

20,000 Persian light cavalry, again mainly javelin-armed, with a sword as a backup. They would not have been armoured. Perhaps a sizeable proportion of these would have been horse archers, made up of Scythians, Sacae and Parthians.

200 heavy chariots, heavy four-horse vehicles. The driver would whip the horses into a frenzy and dive out before they ran into a block of the enemy. Darius had ordered the plain flattened to facilitate their use, but they failed to have much effect; the drivers were always inclined to leap out too early, and were in any case vulnerable to enemy fire from skirmishers. Also, Alexander's infantry were ordered to open their ranks to let the chariots through, which they did, and then re-formed to continue the attack.

15 Indian Elephants, with two men sitting astride each animal's back. There was no tower or howdah. These played no significant part in the battle.

TELAMON 225 BC

Telamon was one of the bloodiest battles of Italian antiquity. The body count was huge, the Gauls reportedly losing 40,000 dead and 10,000 captured soldiers in one day.

BACKGROUND

The Gauls and Romans had a long history of conflict, punctuated by periods of relative harmony. The Gallic/Celtic tribes migrated into Northern Italy in the late fifth and early fourth centuries BC. In 390 BC there was a major struggle for dominance between the two powers in Italy and the Gauls sacked the city of Rome itself. For many centuries after, the Romans retained a collective fear of hordes of barbarians swarming down from the north to attack them.

According to the Greek historian Polybius (c. 200–c. 118 BC), the Romans believed that they would never be safe while the Gauls threatened their northern frontier. The Romans colonized land in the Po Valley in 232 BC. The Gauls in northern Italy became convinced that the Romans were not only aiming for supremacy in Italy but wanted to destroy them completely. They decided to take pre-emptive action.

In 225 BC, a huge Gallic army drawn from the tribes of Cisalpine Gaul (that part of Gaul on the Italian side of the Alps), with a mercenary force from Transalpine Gaul, swarmed southwards through Etruria, annihilating a Roman force at Clusium (Chiusi) 85 miles (3 days' march) north of Rome.

The Roman response was speedy and effective. One of the two serving consuls, L. Aemilius Papus, who had been awaiting the Gallic onslaught at Arminium, marched his army towards Clusium, forcing the Gauls to try to escape north, up the west coast of Italy. The other consul, C. Atilius Regulus, who had been in Sardinia, crossed with his legions to Pisa to try to cut off any possibility of the Gauls retreating. Thus the Gauls found themselves surrounded by two Roman armies at Telamon, on the coast of what is now Tuscany.

THE GALLIC TRIBES

The army of the Gauls was a coalition of Gallic tribes in Northern Italy (the Boii, Insubres, Taurini and Lingones), assisted by mercenaries from Transalpine Gaul (the Gaesatae). The Cisalpine Gallic tribes occupied the plains of the middle and upper Po; the Gaesatae were from the Rhone valley. The Gallic tribes were commanded at Telamon by the kings Anerostes and Concolitanus.

THE GALLIC ARMY

According to Polybius the constant threat from the Gauls throughout the fourth and third centuries BC was a formative influence on the development of Roman military competence. In his view the Romans were level-headed, efficient and dogged: the Gauls were volatile, unpredictable, fierce in their initial onslaught but liable to lose heart and panic. The Gauls were often portrayed by Romans as 'noble savages'.

Modern scholars suggest that the most commonly used weapons among the Gauls were swords, usually fastened on the right side, and spears, for throwing or thrusting. Some Gauls used bows and arrows (although archery was never particularly popular in the Celtic cultures), slings or throwing clubs. Generally Roman troops were better equipped than the Gallic; the Gauls wore little armour apart from shields, sometimes helmets, and occasionally chain mail, although they did wear a torque – a metal collar or neck chain – in battle. The torque had a religious significance, perhaps giving the wearer a sense of being protected by the gods. A number of ancient sources agree in saying that at least some of the Gallic warriors fought naked.

Besides infantry, the Gauls also used agile, fast chariots. Caesar, describing Celtic chariots in Britain almost 200 years later, wrote that in using chariots both the fighting power of infantry and the mobility of cavalry were combined. They acted as mobile missile platforms and transport for elite warriors on the battlefield.

From all that we know, it seems that fighting was part and parcel of Celtic society, but it was limited to individual heroes. These men allowed the whole society to take a vicarious part in battle. Individual warriors would be chosen to fight to the death as representatives for different factions, allowing anger to be satisfied by proxy. Diodorus Siculus, for instance, records that when the Gauls went to battle the chiefs would stand in front of the line and shout at their opponents, challenging the bravest of them to single combat, at the same time waving their weapons to terrify them. When someone accepted a challenge, the chiefs loudly recited the brave deeds of their ancestors, adding the worst insults they could devise about their opponents, in the hope of robbing them of their fighting spirit. The Gauls also often took into battle companions,

whom they called parasites, who would shout their praises before the assembly and the chieftains.

TACTICS OF THE GAULS

The strength of a Gallic attack lay in the first onslaught, its power fuelled by belief in a glorious afterlife, desire for fame, and a hysteria fuelled by noise, chanting and often enhanced by alcohol. Such charges lacked focus and, if repulsed, the Gauls had no strategy for recovery and became desparate. Polybius notes that at Telamon, as the battle turned in the Romans' favour, some Gauls were so distressed that they rushed wildly on the enemy and sacrificed their lives, while others retreated, trampling on those behind who were still advancing. The Romans' chief advantage was their ability to reinforce the parts of their line that were threatened. Gallic armies did sometimes successfully ambush Roman armies, but only when they had time to muster along the route of the Roman march, and they were slow to manoeuvre.

Experts have concluded that the battle of Telamon was the last recorded use of the chariot in battle on the European continent. During the third century BC cavalry became more significant in Gallic warfare. The Gauls had a strong equestrian culture, and soon after this battle their cavalry would be much sought after as mercenary troops for foreign armies; Hannibal, for example, employed them against Rome in his Italian campaigns of 218 BC onwards. Telamon may have been a new development: cavalry played a significant part in the battle but chariots, they seem not to have played an important role.

THE GAESATAE

According to Polybius the mercenary Gaesatae (i.e., probably, 'spearmen') fought naked at Telamon, standing proudly in front of the whole army with nothing but their weapons to protect them. He thought they did so because clothing would be a hindrance in battle; part of the ground was overgrown with brambles that would have caught on their clothes and prevented them using their weapons efficiently. That may, however, be a rationalization: their nudity may simply have been a way of trying to say they were outrageously brave. The Insubres and Boii, by contrast, wore trousers and light cloaks.

THE ROMAN ARMY

The Roman forces at Telamon were commanded by the consuls L. Aemilius Papus and C. Atilius Regulus. The consuls were typically politicians who had received no formal training as generals but usually had extensive military experience; they came, moreover, from a society that prized military ability. At Telamon one consul controlled legions I and III; the other, legions II and IV. The Roman army was not at this date a professional force but was raised annually from the Roman citizenry. Military service was compulsory, all male citizens between the ages of 17 and 46 being required to serve a minimum of six years.

THE ROMAN LEGION

The main unit of the army was the legion, recruited from Roman citizens who were sufficiently wealthy to equip themselves. It consisted of five elements:
✝ cavalry (*equites*): 300 men in ten troops (*turmae*) of 30, each *turma* commanded by three decurions. Roman cavalry were of fairly poor quality, because there was not a strong cavalry tradition in the Roman army.
✝ the first line of heavy infantry (*hastati*): 1,200 men in ten maniples of 120. These were armed with *pila* (the *pilum* is a heavy javelin designed to penetrate the target's shield and armour), swords, shields, helmets and body armour. These men were the youngest.
✝ the second line of heavy infantry (*principes*): 1,200 men in ten maniples of 120, armed with *pila*, swords, shields, helmets and body armour.
✝ the third line of heavy infantry (*triarii*): 600 men in

ten maniples of 60, armed with spears, swords, shields, helmets and body armour. These men were the oldest and most experienced veterans. In all three lines of heavy infantry, the helmet was of bronze and the shield long and cylindrical, constructed of plywood covered with calfskin.
✝ the light infantry (*velites*): 1,200 men who fought in small groups but for administrative purposes were attached to the maniples. Each man was armed with a bundle of javelins and, at least by the early second century BC, a short stabbing sword (*gladius*) and carried a small circular shield.

ALLIES

Each legion was accompanied by a similarly sized unit of Latin and Italian allies. Such an allied unit was called an *ala* (plural: *alae*) or wing, because it was usually deployed on the flanks of the legions. The *alae* appear to have had a similar internal organization and tactical system to the legions.

ROMAN TACTICS

The cavalry tended to be massed on the flanks. The light infantry supported them or were deployed ahead of the main lines. The three lines of heavy infantry were always deployed one behind the other, *hastati* in front, *principes* in the middle and *triarri* in the rear. The ten maniples in each line were deployed side by side with intervals between them equal to the frontage of a maniple. The line behind was staggered so that its maniples covered the gaps between the maniples of the line ahead. This was the famous quincunx, or checkerboard formation. Each maniple was an independent unit commanded by its senior centurion. At times orders might be given to an entire line to advance or retreat. In most circumstances a line was capable only of going forwards or backwards. It was very difficult to manoeuvre the entire line, for instance to wheel it to face a new direction; that would require

CONSULS

The office of consul was evolved after the fall of the Roman kingship in c. 509 BC. There were always two consuls, representing the highest rank of magistrates in the Roman Republic, their joint role equivalent to the rule of a king but without the attendant problems of tyranny, competition and lack of accountability. The consuls were elected by a committee of the people of Rome, the *Comitia Centuriata*, after their names had been put forward by the Senate, and they held the office only for a year. Each consul had the power of veto over the activities of the other. The consuls were in charge of the army, they called the Senate and other assemblies of the people together and they represented the people of Rome in dealings with other states. At first they often came from wealthy families, but a decree of 367 BC stipulated that at least one consul should be a commoner. Once their terms of office expired, many consuls went on to become governors of Roman provinces, a career that could prove very lucrative.

The office of consul remained after the fall of the republic c. 27 BC, but the appointment of consuls passed from the people to the emperor.

giving individual orders to each centurion in charge of a maniple. Essentially the legion of 30 maniples was very good at attacking to its front but had difficulty in doing anything else, or unexpectedly changing the direction of its advance.

Roman armies were known for not taking reconnaissance very seriously. In the ancient world, when fairly small armies marched against each other from long distances, one side would seldom know the other's whereabouts until they were quite close to each other.

PRELUDE TO BATTLE

The Gauls engaged with a Roman advance force at Clusium; their numbers and courage prevailed, about 6,000 Romans were killed and the rest of the Roman army fled to a nearby hilltop. The Gauls attempted to besiege them but tired of this strategy by nightfall. They left a detachment of cavalry to guard the camp and went to their rest, intending to continue the siege the next day.

L. Aemilius, commanding two Roman legions near the Adriatic, had received the news that the Gauls had invaded and had hurried to meet them. At daybreak the next day he ordered his infantry out to meet the Gauls, while he himself led his cavalry towards the besieged hill. The Gauls, however, deciding that they had enough booty and did not want to risk an open battle with the Romans, had broken camp just before daybreak and retreated along the sea-coast through Etruria. Aemilius, having gathered the survivors of the advance force and and united them with his own troops, decided to follow the enemy's rear until the time was right, rather than risk open battle.

Meanwhile C. Atilius, the other consul, also commanding two legions, reached Pisa from Sardinia, marching south towards the northbound Gauls, who were unaware of his presence. When the Gauls neared Telamon in Etruria, their advance troops encountered

ROMAN ARMY

Polybius puts the total Roman forces at 22,000 legionaries and 64,000 light infantry and cavalry, giving a total of 86,000 men. A more likely figure is about 46,000.

Each legion had a total of 4,200 infantry and 300 cavalry. In times of particular crisis the number of infantry might be increased to 5,000 but without varying the number of the triarii.

Cavalry (*equites*): 300 horsemen, divided into ten troops (*turmae*) of 30, each *turma* commanded by three decurions.

Heavy infantry: the youngest soldiers (*hastati*) formed the front line, behind them came the men in their 20s and 30s (*principes*) and in the rear were the older veterans (*triarii*). All wore bronze helmets, and carried long cylindrical body shields constructed of plywood covered with calf skin.

Light infantry (*velites*): normally there were 1,200 of these in a legion. Each man was armed with a bundle of javelins and, at least by the early second century BC, a short stabbing sword (*gladius*) and carried a small circular shield.

The officers – 60 centurions and 30 decurions – were overseen by six military tribunes, two of whom, in rotation, took overall command. A consul was normally given an army of two legions.

ROMAN ALLIED TROOPS

In addition to the Roman legions each army included a similarly sized contingent of allies. About 5,000 infantry, divided into ten cohorts, and 500 cavalry formed an *ala*, commanded by officers known as prefects, who were invariably Romans. The structure of the *ala* mimicked that of the legion. In battle a consular army formed with the two *alae* on either side of a centre composed of Roman legions.

It would seem that the bulk of the allied forces were drawn from the Latin colonies spread throughout Italy. As far as we can tell, they were organized and equipped more or less identically to the Romans, and their own distinctive arms and tactics were absorbed.

GALLIC ARMY

The strength of the Gallic army has been estimated at about 60,000 men.

The basic equipment of a Gallic warrior consisted of a set of one to four spears of varying lengths and a large, leather-covered shield, usually oval in shape, about 1.2m high and 0.5m wide, with a metal shield boss or central stud. With this equipment most warriors wore their everyday clothing of trousers, shirt and mantle, or cloak. Gallic nobles wore torques (neck rings) and carried long swords with blades of about 0.8 to 1 metre long. Noble warriors probably also wore armour and a helmet, both made from leather, or, if they were very rich, a helmet of bronze or iron, elaborately decorated with ornamentation and inlay of coral or even gold.

Sources of the period describe the Gauls as appearing very tall compared to the Romans. They had white skin and fair hair. Some shaved off their beards, but others let them grow moderately. The nobles shaved their cheeks but let their moustaches grow freely so as to cover their mouths. When they ate, the moustaches become mixed with food. The Gauls also used to smear their hair with limewater and pull it back to the top of their head to produce something like a horse's mane.

The Gaesatae, who fought naked, were tall, with large physiques, which they adorned with gold torques and armlets. They were all infantry, a warrior band of mainly young men with a charismatic leader, and were used as intensive fighting troops.

The Insubres and the Boii (and others) were tribes from Cisalpine Gaul (northern Italy), who wore trousers and light cloaks. At the battle of Cannae, nine years later, they wore short, dazzling white linen tunics lined with purple. Countless horns and trumpeters accompanied the Celtic war group.

Atilius' advance guard and were made prisoners. They informed Atilius of the battle and the retreat from Clusium. The Gauls were now caught on the march between two armies. Atilius ordered his tribunes to put the legions in fighting order and to advance at marching pace until they came to ground which allowed them to attack in good formation. He noticed a hill above the road, which the Gauls coming north from Clusium would have to pass, and led his cavalry there.

The main Gallic army was ignorant of the arrival of Atilius' army, so when its soldiers saw his cavalry they assumed that they belonged to Aemilius, who must have passed their flank in the night and occupied the hill. They therefore sent their own cavalry and some of their light-armed troops to try to take the hill. Quickly discovering the presence of Atilius' army, they deployed their infantry facing both forwards and back.

Aemilius knew that Atilius' legions had landed at Pisa but not that they had arrived at the battle, until he saw the fighting for occupation of the hill. He sent his cavalry to help the Romans on the hill, then deployed his infantry in the usual way and advanced against the Gauls.

The Gauls' rearward-facing line, anticipating Aemilius, had the Gaesatae in front and the Insubres behind them. Facing the opposite direction, ready to meet Atilius, were the Taurisci and Boii.

THE COURSE OF THE BATTLE

At first the battle took place only on the hill, with most of the forces only spectators. Atilius was killed and his head brought to the Gallic kings, but after a long and bitter fight the Roman cavalry took possession of the hill.

The Gallic and Roman infantry formations now closed on each other. According to Polybius, onlookers could not tell if the Gauls were helped or hindered by the situation. They were fighting against two enemies at once and at the same time protecting their rear –

but they had no prospect of retreat should they lose. The Romans were encouraged by having caught the Gauls between two armies, but were also terrified by the size, appearance and noise made by their enemies.

The Roman light infantry (*velites*) advanced as usual from the ranks of the legions, their javelins inflicting heavy damage on the naked Gaesatae. Unable to stop this attack, some of the Gaesatae sacrificed themselves by rushing at the enemy. Others retreated step-by-step, throwing the ranks of the troops behind them into disorder.

Having overcome the Gaesatae, the *velites* withdrew into their ranks and the Roman heavy infantry attacked the Insubres, Boii and Taurisci behind them. Stubborn hand-to-hand combat ensued, resulting in carnage. The Gauls held their ground, though suffering heavy losses, because their weapons were inferior to the Romans', but they were finally defeated when they were attacked on their flank by the Roman cavalry, riding down the hill and into them. The Gallic infantry were cut to pieces, and the Gallic cavalry fled.

AFTERMATH

The Gallic king Concolitanus was taken prisoner. King Anerostes escaped with some of his followers, but they all committed suicide together soon afterwards, following the practice of a Gallic loyalty cult in which dedicated bands surrounded kings and swore to follow them even to death.

The surviving Roman consul, Aemilius, pursued the Boii into their own territory in northern Italy and the following year both consuls forced this tribe into submission. In 223 and 222 BC, the consuls of those years attacked the Insubres even further into Gallic territory and subdued them.

In short, the Gauls lost control of northern Italy, which became the Roman province of Cisalpine Gaul. The Roman frontier in Italy now reached to the Alps.

the gauls at war

The classic Roman view of the Gallic warrior comes from the Greek geographer and historian Strabo (64/63 BC–after AD 23). 'The whole race is madly fond of war, high spirited and quick to battle, but otherwise straightforward and not of evil character. And so when they are stirred up they assemble in their bands for battle, quite openly and without forethought, so that they are easily handled by those who desire to outwit them.' When they are aroused 'they are ready to face danger even if they have nothing on their side but their own strength and courage . . . their strength depends on their mighty bodies, and on their numbers . . . to the frankness and high-spiritedness of their temperament must be added the traits of childish boastfulness and love of decoration. They wear ornaments of gold torques on their necks, and bracelets on their arms and wrists, while people of high rank wear dyed garments besprinkled with gold. It is this vanity which makes them unbearable in victory and so completely downcast in defeat.'

The Gauls made much use of psychological warfare, in two ways. Before a battle they would create an enormous amount of noise by clashing their weapons against their shields, shouting and singing; trumpeters would blow and drums might be beaten. A second weapon was verbal display: before battle, the leaders would parade in front of their troops, performing heroic feats, proclaiming their own deeds, belittling their enemies and challenging opposing leaders to duels.

It was also Gallic practice to behead those one conquered in battle and to tie the head to one's saddle.

There are several representations of Gallic trumpets in ancient sculpture, particularly at Pergamon in Asia Minor and on the triumphal arch at Orange in southern France, and a few fragments of actual trumpets have survived. A trumpet's mouth, shaped like a boar's head, was found in 1816 at Deskford in Banffshire, in the Grampian region of Scotland. The remainder of the instrument is lost, but the mouth may be compared with images on a cauldron from Gundestrup in Denmark, where the trumpet's sectional construction is clearly shown. The Deskford trumpet may originally have had ears and a mane rather like the Gundestrup examples. When first discovered, it still had a movable wooden 'tongue', which may have added vibration to the strident sounds blown from it. The Deskford piece is usually dated to the middle of the first century AD. Among earlier representations of trumpets are those in the temple of Athena Polias Nikephoros at Pergamon, dated 181 BC and celebrating the victories of Attalus I over the Galatian tribes in the late third century BC. On the triumphal arch at Orange, trumpets, shields, standards, indeed all the trophies are set out in a great display of spoils of war. The large number of trumpets supports the descriptions of great noise during battle reported by the classical writers.

TREBIA DECEMBER 218 BC

BACKGROUND

The battle of Trebia was the first major confrontation in the second of three long wars between Rome and the Carthaginians of North Africa. Because Carthage was founded by the Phoenicians, a Semitic people from the coast of what is now Lebanon, whom the Romans called *Poeni*, these have come to be known as the Punic Wars.

By the fifth century BC Carthage had built a large trading empire centred on North Africa and the Mediterranean, including the entire North African coast, southern Spain, Corsica, Sardinia and Sicily. With Rome expanding into the region by the third century BC, it was inevitable there would be conflict between the two powers. The First Punic War (264–241 BC) began with a dispute between them over Sicily. In 264 the Carthaginians established a presence on the island, to which the Romans retaliated in 260 by sending a fleet there, which also expelled the Carthaginians from Corsica but failed to gain total control of Sicily. The struggle for control of Sicily continued until 241 when a Roman fleet of 200 warships gave them control of the sea lanes and forced the collapse of the Carthaginian stronghold in Sicily.

As part of continued expansion in the Mediterranean, Hamilcar Barca, Hannibal's father, invaded southern Spain in 237 BC and founded a new capital at Cartago Nova (now Cartagena). By 219 BC, Hannibal, taking up his father's mantle, had captured Saguntum, a city with which, according to a treaty signed between Rome and Carthage immediately after the First Punic War, the Romans had 'friendship'. The Romans took this attack as an act of war and demanded that Hannibal be surrendered to them.

Coming from a family of successful Carthaginian generals, Hannibal had learned to hate Rome at an early age. It is reported that as a boy his father bound him with a solemn promise 'never to be a friend to the Romans'. Anti-Roman feeling in Carthage was ignited by its defeat in the First Punic War and fanned by Rome's aggressive and expansionist behaviour towards it ever since.

Hannibal spent the winter of 219–218 BC at Cartagena, finalizing his plans and bringing together all the men and equipment he would need to realize his great strategic insight, that to attack Rome effectively it was necessary to strike directly at the city and state of Rome itself. Roman control of the seas was absolute, so the only way to achieve this aim was to march by land into Italy.

In April/May of 218 BC, therefore, Hannibal marched his army across the River Ebro in northern Spain and headed towards what is now southern France. According to Polybius, the army consisted of 90,000 infantry and 12,000 cavalry. Modern authorities put the figure nearer 40,000. The indigenous tribes of the Pyrenees harried the army as it marched north, and some of Hannibal's Spanish troops deserted. Nonetheless, he reached the River Rhône. P. Cornelius Scipio, whose army had been detained in northern Italy by a rebellion, landed his legions at Massilia (Marseilles) and pursued Hannibal up the Rhône. Then, evidently realizing that Hannibal intended to enter Italy across the Alps, he decided to return to Italy and wait for him there.

CROSSING THE ALPS

Historians have argued for centuries about the precise route that Hannibal followed across the Alps into northern Italy. Hannibal seems to have made contact, while in southern France, with the northern Italian tribe of the Boii, who would have had detailed knowledge of Alpine routes into Italy and probably gave Hannibal considerable help in deciding how to proceed.

Hannibal's crossing of the Alps is one of the great epics of human history. His army was attacked by Gallic tribes such as the Allobroges; other tribes rolled heavy stones down on to them as they picked their way through the mountains. Snow and ice at the summits of the passes turned a difficult journey into a nightmare, as heavily laden men and animals, including elephants, slithered and slipped down icy slopes covered with fresh snow. It is estimated that the crossing took 15 days and that Hannibal lost perhaps half of his entire army. Five months after he left Spain, he finally arrived in the upper Po valley.

Hannibal's troops were loyal not simply to Carthaginian causes but to the general himself. He was not afraid to take calculated risks, he was able to inspire and unify an army from several different countries and he was a master of strategy, winning decisive victories over the Romans even while on their territory and vastly outnumbered.

Scipio, having returned to Italy, rushed his army to the Po valley to protect the new Roman colonies of Placentia (Piacenza) and Cremona. The armies first clashed near the River Ticinum (Ticino). For Hannibal to refuse battle at this point was impossible, despite the gruelling experience his army had just been through. In order to defeat the Romans he needed the support of the local tribes, and to refuse battle might have seemed a sign of weakness.

The encounter at Ticinus was more a cavalry engagement than a full-scale pitched battle. Both leaders brought out their cavalry divisions, which clashed with each other chaotically. Hannibal prevailed by keeping back his Numidian cavalry, which engaged the Romans on their flank and put them to flight.

Scipio was severely wounded and, legend has it, was saved from death by his own son. He withdrew to Placentia, where his foes followed him a few days later. Hannibal drew up his forces in battle order, but the Romans did nothing, remaining within their camp. Hannibal then began to make alliances among the surrounding Gallic tribes.

HANNIBAL'S CAVALRY

Hannibal's cavalry were his most important units. He often used his light Numidian cavalry to goad the Romans into battle before they were ready. The Numidians, who were among the finest horsemen of the ancient world, rode without saddles and armour. At Trebia they positioned themselves just outside the Roman camp and taunted the Romans with insults, goading them into battle whilst they were still encamped.

ELEPHANTS

Trebia is the only battle Hannibal fought in Italy with elephants. He probably had about 30, having started his journey with 37. Each elephant probably carried on its back a tower with a javelineer on top. Elephants were risky weapons. On the one hand, they shocked and frightened the Romans, who had not encountered them in battle for at least 40 years, and probably never on their own soil; but, if they panicked, they could be as dangerous to their own army as to the enemy. Scholars suggest that Hannibal's elephants' drivers now carried a recent invention, a spiked blade that they could hammer into an elephant's brain to kill it.

THE ROMAN ARMY

Military service was compulsory at this time for all male Roman citizens between the age of 17 and 24, who were required to serve a minimum of 6 years. Thus the Roman army was not a professional army at this stage. The legion was the main unit of the army, and consisted of five elements:

† the first line of heavy infantry: these were armed with *pila*, swords, shields, helmets and body armour.
† the second line of heavy infantry: 1,200 men armed with *pila*, swords, shields, helmets and body armour.
† the third line of heavy infantry: 600 men armed with spears, swords, shields, helmets and body armour.
† the light infantry (*velites*): 1,200 men armed with a bundle of javelins and a short stabbing sword (*gladius*) and a small circular shield.
† cavalry (*equites*): 300 men in ten troops (*turmae*) of 30, each *turma* commanded by three decurions.

ROMAN TACTICS

The cavalry of the entire army was generally massed on the flanks with the light infantry either supporting them or deployed ahead of the main lines. It was extremely difficult to manoeuvre the entire line as this would require giving individual orders to each centurion. The legion was very good at attacking to its front but had difficulty in doing anything else.

PRELUDE TO BATTLE

After the battle at Ticinus, Hannibal had given his troops time to rest and find food, so that they were well prepared for another encounter. His defeat of Scipio had encouraged the local Gallic tribes, who now gathered around him, increasing his force. He had also scouted out the next battlefield, a plain west of the river Trebia, towards Placentia, where Scipio's camp was.

Having carefully viewed the area, Hannibal took advantage of the natural features and placed an ambush force, consisting of 1,000 Numidian cavalry and 1,000 infantry under command of his brother Mago, on the steep banks of a watercourse south of where he expected to lure the Romans to fight. They were instructed to stay there, under the cover of bushes, and emerge at a crucial point of the battle.

When they heard of Hannibal's departure from northern Spain, the Romans had panicked and dispatched armies to Spain and Sicily, but once it was known that Hannibal was in Italy, the Senate recalled the army bound for Sicily. Under the command of Sempronius Longus, they succeeded in reaching Scipio's camp within 40 days of passing Rome. The Romans could now bring the strength of a full consular army to bear on Hannibal's forces, together with the remainder of the force that Scipio had commanded at Ticinus.

Sempronius Longus was keen to join battle with Hannibal, but Scipio was reluctant. It has been suggested that he argued for delay, saying that it would weaken Hannibal and strengthen the Romans. There may have been some grounds for that belief, because Hannibal had brought with him a force that, even before the gruelling Alpine crossing, was made up of experienced soldiers, while the Roman army was inexperienced and vulnerable. A month or so of further training might well have been to the Roman army's advantage. Another important element in Scipio's thinking may have been the weather. It was December, the temperature had fallen and the area was covered with snow and ice.

TROOPS AT TREBIA

ROMAN ARMY — TOTAL 45,000

Roman legions I to IV – 16,000 heavy infantry
Roman cavalry – 1,000
Roman light infantry skirmishers (*velites*) – 3,000
Allied heavy infantry – 20,000
Allied light infantry skirmishers – 2,000
Allied cavalry – 3,000

THE CARTHAGINIAN ARMY – TOTAL 39,030

Elephants – 30
Numidian light cavalry – 2,000
Gallic heavy cavalry – 4,000
Spanish (Iberian) heavy cavalry – 3,000
Libyan heavy infantry – 10,000
Gallic heavy infantry – 8,000
Spanish (Iberian) heavy infantry – 2,000
Light armed spear-bearers (skirmishers) – 6,000
Balearic slingers (skirmishers) – 2,000
Plus the ambush force under Mago of 1,000
Numidian Cavalry and 1,000 Infantry

THE COURSE OF THE BATTLE

In the event, Scipio would not be allowed to wait; Hannibal was determined to fight. Early one morning he dispatched a group of 1,000 cavalry and 1,000 infantry towards the Roman camp. This force harassed and attacked the outskirts of the camp, until Sempronius Longus, caught off-guard, hastily assembled the whole Roman army and set it marching immediately towards the River Trebia in pursuit.

Livy, the famous Roman historian of the first century BC, tells us in his *History of Rome* that Hannibal's army had lit fires that morning, eaten well and oiled their bodies against the cold. The Roman army, on the other hand, had been hurled into action without eating anything. Having marched steadily without food, the Romans were confronted by the ice-cold River Trebia, with Hannibal's army on the farther shore. Slowly and laboriously they crossed the river, and, when they assembled in battle formation in front of Hannibal's army, they were frozen, soaked and very hungry.

Hannibal's battle order placed his heavily armed infantry in the centre of the field, behind a screen of 8,000 light infantry. On the wings were 10,000 cavalry, with his elephants divided between the extreme ends of the wings. Sempronius arranged his four legions, comprising about 16,000 Roman troops and 20,000 allies, in the standard three-line formation of the time, with 4,000 cavalry and about 3,000 Cenomanians, Gallic tribesmen who had remained loyal to Rome, on the flanks.

The Roman light infantry's shower of javelins proved ineffective, and they were pulled back. The Roman cavalry then came under attack from the javelins of Hannibal's heavy infantry and his elephants. The Roman cavalry horses, unused to elephants, panicked and turned the event into a rout. The Roman heavy infantry, despite their cold and hunger, managed to hold their own with Hannibal's heavy infantry and might have prevailed. Hannibal's

elephants, however, now began to attack the Roman centre. It was at this point that Hannibal gave the signal for Mago and his concealed group to attack. They poured out of their hiding place, creating slaughter and devastation in the Roman rear.

Despite this very difficult situation, the Romans continued for a while to hack their way into the Carthaginian lines. In Livy's description of the battle the Romans even succeeded in coping with Hannibal's elephants, stabbing and thrusting at them with javelins on their undersides, where the skin was softest. Hannibal then moved the elephants back out to the wings, where they succeeded once more in creating devastation. The Romans were being forced to fight in what amounted to a circle and, by sheer determination, 10,000 legionaries carved their way through the Carthaginian centre. By this point in the battle, says Livy, heavy rain was falling, which made it impossible for those legionaries who had succeeded in penetrating the Carthaginian centre to see how they could regroup and return to the battle to help their fellows. They therefore made for Placentia, but many were pushed back to the Trebia, where they drowned, were killed in the shallows or, fearing to cross the river, were cut off in pockets and killed. The combination of very cold snow and rain killed many men and horses, and almost wiped out the elephants.

The Carthaginians did not pursue the Romans farther than the river but returned to their camp, so numbed by cold that they could feel no pleasure in their victory. Perhaps their exhaustion prevented them noticing that, the night after the battle, many Romans got away down the river on rafts, though it is also possible that the Romans' escape was muffled by the noise of the rain. Scipio led his troops to Placentia and then crossed the Po to Cremona, perhaps realizing that having two armies foraging for food in winter in one small area could make keeping his forces alive very difficult indeed.

AFTERMATH

It has been estimated that up to 15,000 or even 20,000 Romans were killed at Trebia, while the Carthaginian losses were small. One immediate result of the defeat was that Hannibal attracted strong support from the Gallic tribes of northern Italy. In the spring of 217 BC he was able to advance as far south as the River Arno. By that time, two full Roman armies were in the field, looking for the opportunity to destroy him and his army.

Hannibal first outmanoeuvred the army of C. Flaminius at Arretium, then brought it to battle in a carefully planned trap at Lake Trasimene, where the Roman force was all but annihilated. Hannibal did not, however, then advance on Rome. He withdrew to Picenum to rest, and later ravaged Apulia and Campania.

ELEPHANTS USED IN WAR

Elephas maximus asurus lived in Iran and Syria. Early drawings of the animal and fragmentary skeletal remains indicate that it was the largest subspecies of the Asian elephant. The war elephants employed by the Greek king Pyrrhus in his battles with Rome, and engraved upon Roman seals, show animals of unusual size. 'Sarus' ('the Syrian') was the outstanding animal in Hannibal's elephant battle squadron.

Alexander the Great encountered elephants in his campaigns in India, and his successors incorporated them into their armies. Elephants were imported from India from the late fourth century BC onwards for use in war. Alexander's successors in the Middle East, the Seleucid dynasty, had their own stud farms and bred elephants for war.

Polybius gives a vivid description of how elephants fought each other: 'With their tusks firmly interlocked, they shove with all their might, each trying to force the other to give ground, until the one who proves strongest pushes aside the other's trunk, and then, when he has once made him turn and has him in the flank, he gores him with his tusks as a bull does with his horns.'

Elephants' drivers were vulnerable to missiles. If its driver was killed, or it suffered many pinprick wounds from missiles such as javelins, an elephant might panic and trample anything in its way. Hellenistic armies therefore came to have an escort of light troops to protect them. Elephants were effective weapons against cavalry, because horses were frightened of them, but they were best employed against a stationary enemy.

Anti-elephant devices adopted by Hellenistic armies included planting spikes in the ground (this seems to have been the most effective) or an opposing force of elephants.

Between the First and Second Punic Wars, the Roman Senate was most concerned with the problem of subduing the Gallic tribes, particularly those in Cisalpine Gaul. After the battle of Telamon, a number of consular armies were sent against the Gauls to subdue them; they were successful, and all the Gallic tribes surrendered. Two new Roman colonies were established in Cisalpine Gaul. The presence of these new settlements, situated further north than ever before and in prime farming land, was a constant source of friction between the Romans and the Gauls, and the bitterness and resentment they caused meant that any peace between them would be short-lived.

In 218 BC a rebellion duly broke out in Cisalpine Gaul. The Boii and Insubres drove the settlers from the two new colonies to the city of Mutina, which they then besieged. A relief column of Roman soldiers was ambushed and suffered heavy losses.

Meanwhile Hannibal was preparing his invasion of Italy and sent envoys to the Gallic tribes to seek support. The tribes' recent memories of heavy losses at the hands of the Romans, particularly at Telamon, made them receptive to Hannibal's overtures. Hannibal arrived in northern Italy in the territory of the Taurini, with whom he does not seem to have had previous contact. They did not receive him favourably, so he besieged their main hill town and, after three days, stormed it and, in a calculated display of strength, massacred the inhabitants. He then learned that Scipio commanded a Roman force near the head of the Po Valley. The presence of such a strong Roman force deterred the Gallic tribes there, the Boii and Insubres, from joining him.

In November 218 there was a small battle between some of the Roman forces under Scipio and some of Hannibal's army. Scipio suffered heavy losses and retreated. Hannibal followed him and challenged the Romans to an open battle near the River Ticinus. The Romans refused. Now confident, Hannibal set up camp only five or six miles away. This demonstration of Roman weakness had an effect on the Gallic allies in the Roman camp, and during the night a group of them massacred and beheaded the soldiers sleeping near them and deserted to Hannibal. The deserters numbered 200 cavalry and 2,000 infantry. Hannibal welcomed them, promising them rich rewards and sending them back to their own tribes to muster further support.

That was the turning point in Hannibal's dealings with the Gallic tribes. Chieftains from the Boii arrived in his camp, bringing the Romans whom they had captured in their attack on the Roman colonies earlier in the year. Hannibal now made a formal alliance with the tribe. The full battle of the River Ticinus followed and Hannibal won.

RAPHIA 22 JUNE 217 BC

This Egyptian victory forced the Seleucid Empire to give back the whole of Coele-Syria (Phoenicia, Philistia and southern Syria – or modern Israel, Palestine and Lebanon). Since their creation, soon after the death of Alexander the Great, the two empires had hotly disputed this territory. Geographically it was the all-important borderland that separated them, but it also brought control of crucial ports on the Mediterranean, and of the mountains inland.

BACKGROUND

Despite his death over 100 years before, Raphia – and indeed the entire Hellenistic Age – must be understood in the light of the legacy of Alexander the Great. Upon his sudden death in 323 BC, Alexander's empire was left in the hands of his rival generals. Perhaps inevitably, one of the greatest periods of conquest in history was followed by one of the most spectacular periods of rivalry, division and strife. Alexander's empire was dismantled as quickly as it had been amassed, as these generals contested and divided the conquered lands between themselves. By the dawn of the third century BC, they had established certain regions of control, which effectively became separate kingdoms. At the time of Raphia the three principal powers were the Ptolemaic dynasty in Egypt, the Seleucids in Asia and the Antigonids in Macedonia. Since the Antigonid king Philip V was preoccupied with events in Illyria and Greece, the other two were able to fight each other without fear of an attack from the north.

THE EGYPTIAN EMPIRE UNDER PTOLEMY IV

Ptolemy IV acceded to the Egyptian throne in 221 BC. At that time the Egyptian Empire encompassed what is now Egypt, the North African coast and the Near East (modern Israel, Palestine, and Lebanon). Polybius describes this accession as a crucial moment in the history of the Ptolemies, for it began the decline of their empire. Ptolemy certainly seems to have been decadent, establishing a Dionysian community at his court that was characterized by opulent living and ecstatic worship of the Greek god Dionysus. His empire, however, was not healthy; there was a manpower shortage, and the leading officials at Alexandria, Sosibius and Agathocles, committed a series of murders to safeguard their influence, which presented the Seleucid king Antiochus with an opportune moment to attack. At the battle itself, Ptolemy was accompanied by his sister, who was involved in the crucial whipping up of the phalanx, and whom he married afterwards. His victory at Raphia was perhaps unexpected, given that he was no great general. Polybius criticizes him for not pressing home his advantage over the Seleucids with an invasion of their empire, but the charge is unjust, as it was probably not politically expedient to do so.

THE SELEUCID EMPIRE UNDER ANTIOCHUS III

Antiochus III acceded to the Seleucid throne in 223 BC at the age of 20, following the murder of his brother Seleucus III. He inherited a small empire in Asia (loosely, modern Turkey and the Middle East) that had been weakened by three Syrian Wars with Egypt and the secession in the east of the kingdoms of Bactria and Parthia. Determined to rebuild, Antiochus set out to regain Coele-Syria from the Ptolemies, but soon had to return to deal with Molon, governor of Media, who had rebelled and reneged on his agreements with the Seleucid dynasty. Having settled that business successfully, he then disposed of Hermias, his deeply unpopular chief minister, who had initially held significant influence over him but had subsequently aroused his suspicions. A confident Antiochus then returned to pursue his goals in Coele-Syria. He fell short at Raphia, but eventually gained the territory about two decades later. During that time he also succeeded in repossessing the eastern *satrapies* (governorships) and establishing control of the seaports in the Hellespont, and even led an expedition to India. He longed to emulate Alexander, and in many respects deserved his title of 'Antiochus the Great'.

CAUSES OF THE CONFLICT

The battle of Raphia was part of the ongoing Syrian Wars between the Ptolemies and Seleucids over possession of Coele-Syria. Ptolemy I, after many attempts, had succeeded in establishing dominion over the territory and the Ptolemies managed to hold on to it for a century. However, the settlement between Ptolemy I and Seleucus I in 301 BC technically gave the region to the latter. Seleucus chose not to pursue his rival, who maintained his occupation, but with the accession of a new generation, conflict broke out in the First Syrian War (276–272 BC), the Second, which ended in 258 BC, and the Third, which broke out in 246 BC with the simultaneous accessions of Ptolemy

III and Seleucus II. Raphia was the crucial battle of the Fourth Syrian War.

For both empires, the ports on the Mediterranean coast were important for control of the sea and thus trade, and the mountains and cedars of Lebanon for the supply of timber for boat-building. Also, although they were oriental states, both had a strong psychological attraction to Greece, the Aegean Sea and the Greek coastal cities in western Asia Minor. However, for both empires the importance of Coele-Syria was primarily geopolitical. From the Ptolemaic point of view, it formed a buffer zone between Egypt and the Seleucids and was part of a wider ring of external possessions that surrounded Egypt, including Cyprus, Cyrenaica and territories in western Asia Minor and the Aegean. Crucially, it protected them from invasion from the dangerous northeast. From a Seleucid point of view, a Ptolemaic presence in Coele-Syria was dangerously close to the heart of their empire; in particular, the Ptolemaic occupation of Seleucia, more or less at the gates of the capital, Antioch, must have been a constant provocation.

When Antiochus III took the throne in 223 BC, he was determined to press the Seleucid claim to Coele-Syria. He marched west in 221 BC, but met with resistance from the Ptolemaic general Theodotus in Lebanon and Antilebanon. After attending to his domestic problems, he returned to take advantage of Egypt's weakened state upon the accession of Ptolemy IV. In 219 BC Antiochus took the cities of Seleucia in Prieria and later Tyre and Ptolemais, even persuading some of Ptolemy's troops and generals to defect. The parlous condition of Egypt forced Ptolemy to sue for peace in the winter of 219/18 BC. The negotiations were protracted and, according to Polybius, a stumbling-block insurmountable for both sides soon became apparent: Achaeus, previously governor of Asia Minor. Antiochus refused to allow Ptolemy, as part of any agreement, to take under his wing a man who had rebelled against Seleucid rule in Asia Minor. However, by the beginning of spring 217 BC, Ptolemy was able to engage his enemy with a proper army, mainly because his talented minister Sosibius had successfully addressed the Egyptian manpower crisis by secretly training a force of native Egyptians to supplement Ptolemy's existing forces.

HELLENISTIC WARFARE

Hellenistic armies were essentially similar to the army of Alexander the Great, if modified at times in the light of experience and necessity. The tactical principles in evidence at Raphia were fundamentally the same as those used by the Macedonians at Gaugamela and Issus well over a century earlier. The basic idea was still to pin down the enemy by infantry pressure along much of the line, then deliver a crucial assault at a selected point by means of cavalry. Hence a well-trained phalanx and swift, decisive heavy cavalry were still the prized assets of any Hellenistic army, supplemented by a wide range of light troops.

However, because of manpower shortages and the difficulty of maintaining enough horses, the Hellenistic kingdoms were never able to field enough cavalry, and, by default rather than choice, came to rely more on the phalanx. Pike phalanxes tended to win battles by slowly grinding down the enemy – a war of attrition. Lack of cavalry also rendered the flanks of a phalanx particularly vulnerable.

At Raphia one can deduce the tactical thinking from the battle lines, where cavalry flanked the phalanx on either side, and from the precedent of the Ptolemaic victory at Gaza in 312 BC: the cavalry on each wing would break the enemy cavalry opposite in order to open the enemy phalanx up to flank attacks. In the event, both sides scored a cavalry victory on one wing, but those contests became so far separated from the main phalanxes that neither side could then deploy their victorious cavalry decisively against the enemy infantry, so it was left to the phalanxes to decide the issue by themselves. In any case, as Polybius points out, they were always likely, because of their size, to be the definitive forces in the battle.

One crucial innovation in Hellenistic warfare marked it out from Alexander's era: the widespread use of war elephants, a tactic learned from the Indians. Alexander died soon after his conquests in India and so it was left to his successors to incorporate these beasts into tactical military thinking. They were employed as an ancient equivalent of the tank, in order to assault and disrupt the enemy line. There were several means of preventing this. One was to stop them reaching the line in the first place, which Ptolemy I did very successfully against Demetrius at Gaza in 312 BC. In front of his army he put out a screen of men armed with iron-covered stakes, which were fixed into the ground to block the advancing animals. Another solution, more widely adopted, was to attack the elephants and their drivers with highly mobile light troops armed with javelins or bows. Consequently elephants could advance only with their own lightly armed troops in attendance to neutralize those of the opposition. Yet the major problem for the Ptolemies when using elephants was getting an adequate supply of good-quality animals. They did not have access to Indian elephants – unlike the Seleucids, who bred them on stud farms – and so had to settle for their African counterparts, but the only trainable African elephants were the smaller forest variety, which were ineffective in head-on charges and clashes against the Indian beasts. At Raphia most declined to fight, but fled, 'unable,' as Polybius recounts, 'to stand the smell of and the trumpeting of the Indian elephants, and terrified by their great size and strength'.

Another notable change in Hellenistic armies during the third century BC was the gradual dilution of the Macedonian element. Initially, this was in favour

DECISIVE FACTORS

The most exciting aspect of the battle was the clash of Ptolemy's African elephants and the Indian beasts of Seleucus. Generally the African animals, being smaller, were inclined to retreat from their Indian counterparts. However, as Ptolemy demonstrated on his right wing, skilful manoeuvring with the cavalry could lure the larger Indian elephants out and open up the flank of the Seleucid army.

Yet, in the end, the outcome of the battle rested on the phalanxes. Ptolemy was victorious essentially because he was on hand to inspire his infantrymen from directly behind them, while Antiochus allowed himself to be distracted by his initial success on his right wing. In short, in an intriguing contest of (largely) like versus like, Ptolemy was able to coordinate the various contingents of his army marginally better than Antiochus.

AFTERMATH

Antiochus retired to Raphia, believing he had won the battle because he had been victorious on his own wing, but was soon forced to retreat to his own kingdom, ceding Raphia and indeed the whole of Coele-Syria to Ptolemy. The cities of Coele-Syria, says Polybius, welcomed back Egyptian control with open arms, because they had always preferred that type of government to the Seleucids'. Antiochus, fearful of an invasion from Ptolemy, sent his nephew to sue for peace. Ptolemy, who was never realistically in a position to attack the Seleucid Empire, readily agreed terms.

In the long run, Ptolemy's victory had little lasting effect. The Syrian Wars continued and several years later, in 198 BC, Antiochus III defeated Egypt at the Battle of Paneas. Coele-Syria henceforth became part of the Seleucid kingdom, never to be retrieved by the Egyptians.

DEFENCE AGAINST ELEPHANTS

Confronting a massive elephant on the battlefield and, if possible, repelling its attack requires considerable planning. Foot soldiers can try to work their way under the animal and stab it from below with javelins and swords. Alternatively, one could attack the men who guided the elephants (*mahouts*), because an elephant without a driver is no longer an efficient weapon.

The Roman general Scipio Africanus showed how practice made perfect in defeating elephants. Having had the experience of facing Hannibal's elephants in the battle of Trebia in 218 BC, Scipio developed a clever way to defeat them, and Hannibal, 16 years later at the battle of Zama. When the elephants neared his troop lines, the troops opened pathways between them wide enough for the elephants to be driven down. Then, once the elephants had been chased to the back of the battle line, they were killed with much less risk to the troops.

At the battle of Beneventum in 275 BC, the Romans are said to have defeated the Greek general Pyrrhus' elephants by driving flocks of pigs towards them.

Not surprisingly, Julius Caesar, one of the greatest generals in history, developed a very effective means of neutralizing the threat from elephants. Before the battle of Thapsus in North Africa in 46 BC, he knew that elephants would be used against him by Juba, the king of Numidia. He therefore had elephants – probably veterans of gladiatorial combats – brought from Italy and acclimatized his horses to them by allowing the animals to mix. In doing so he also let his own troops become used to elephants, and evolve tactics for successfully defeating them.

EGYPTIAN ARMY

The Egyptian troops numbered 68,073: 5,000 cavalry; 63,000 infantry; 73 African elephants.

3,000 heavy cavalry, armed with a long spear (*xyston*) perhaps as much as 12 feet in length, which was thrust underarm. After the initial charge, it was broken or dropped, lest the reaction force unseat the rider, who then used a short slashing sword. They did not carry shields, but wore a stiffened linen cuirass and a bronze helmet, which tended to be like the Thracian in shape and crested. They fought in a wedge – a triangular formation with the leader at the point, the apex directed at the enemy – which proved extremely effective in scattering opposing cavalry. Although incapable of a direct attack on enemy heavy infantry, they could easily exploit gaps, making deadly flank or rear attacks. Possibly about 700 of these would have been guard cavalry, the elite of the army – aristocrats obliged to share danger with their king.

2,000 light cavalry, equipped with javelins and swords. The evidence is uncertain, but they probably also carried shields. Included all Greek mercenary cavalry.

28,000 'Macedonian' phalanx, equipped with 21-foot pikes (*sarissae*), backed up by short swords. They were protected by helmets, linen or metal cuirasses and small round shields strapped to the left arm. These troops were highly motivated.

23,000 Egyptian and Libyan phalanx, similarly equipped but serving under different systems of recruitment. They were slighty inferior to the typical Seleucid pikemen. Of this number 3,000 were Libyans and 20,000 Egyptians.

3,000 peltasts, equipped with shields and javelins. Some commentators argue that they had the same equipment as the pikemen, but that would have given little variety to the army.

6,000 Galatians and Thracians, who did not wear armour but carried large shields, javelins and swords and fought *en masse* rather than as skirmishers. Galatians were Gauls who had settled in Asia Minor earlier in the century. Galatians and Thracians were evenly represented.

3,000 Cretan archers, equipped with bows, swords and small shields. They were primarily skirmishers.

73 African elephants, which probably carried a fighting crew of two in a tower as well as a driver. The crew were armoured, but not the driver; their weapons included javelins, pikes and bows. These animals were smaller and usually defeated by Indian elephants in combat.

of mercenaries, but by the time of Raphia native populations made good the losses. Macedonians and their descendants formed a comparatively small proportion of Ptolemy's army; at least 2,000 of his all-important heavy cavalry were Libyans and Egyptians and almost half his phalanx were natives too. Some have argued that this caused problems for Ptolemaic rule in Egypt, since it persuaded native Egyptians of their powers of self-reliance.

TERRAIN

The battlefield was a flat, barren, desert plain. The Seleucids, who controlled the city of Raphia, had marched down the coast past it from the north and set up camp on the plain. The Egyptians approached the battlefield from the west and occupied that side of the plain.

PRELUDE TO BATTLE

From the west, Ptolemy marched into Coele-Syria, setting up camp just before the city of Raphia. Antiochus, marching south down the coast and taking Gaza on his way, took Raphia, marched his troops past the city and encamped on the other side of the plain. A stand-off ensued for five days, during which there were several skirmishes between the two sides' foraging and watering parties and an occasional exchange of missiles between the cavalry and even the infantry.

Ptolemy was the first to move his army out of camp; Antiochus immediately followed suit. Both generals deployed their armies with the phalanx at the centre and cavalry on the wings. In front of each flank both placed elephants – 40 on Ptolemy's left flank and 33 on his right, 60 on Antiochus' right flank and 42 on his left – to screen and break the formation of the charging enemy cavalry. The elephants in turn were supported by archers and peltasts. Ptolemy positioned himself on his right wing, while Antiochus placed himself on his left wing in order to confront his rival directly. Before taking up these positions both generals made speeches to their armies, focusing particularly on their phalanxes as the forces that would bring them victory.

THE COURSE OF THE BATTLE

Battle opened with Antiochus' 60 elephants on his right flank charging Ptolemy's 40 on his left. Ptolemy's smaller African elephants gave way, falling back on their own lines and disturbing the Egyptian left wing. Once the elephants were dealt with, Antiochus rode around Ptolemy's left wing and began attacking it from the flank, putting it to rout. He then chased the fleeing forces off the field of battle.

But Ptolemy had not lost the battle yet. Although his left wing had been swept away, he decided to attack with his right wing. This time he sent out a cavalry force to distract the enemy's elephants. Once these were successfully drawn in, he sent the remainder of the cavalry on his right wing to attack the Seleucid left in the flank and rear, and succeeded in driving Antiochus' left into disarray and retreat. The battle now reached its climax with each right wing having defeated the opposing left wing and pursued it off the field, leaving the phalanxes alone to decide the issue.

As Polybius states, the result turned on the inexperience of Antiochus. Whereas Ptolemy had the foresight to extricate himself from his fleeing wing and position himself behind his phalanx, Antiochus allowed himself to become preoccupied with destroying the enemy left completely. From where Ptolemy was, he could urge his phalanx on. Buoyed by the visible presence of their commander, they levelled their pikes and charged and, after some resistance, broke through the Seleucid ranks. Too late, Antiochus realized what was happening and returned from his pursuit to witness the destruction of his main army.

The Seleucid troops numbered 62,602: 6,000 cavalry; 56,500 infantry (35,000 phalangites and 21,500 light infantry); 102 Indian elephants.

5,000 heavy cavalry, whose armour, weapons and tactics were similar to those of their Egyptian counterparts. They were divided into units of 1,000. Perhaps 2,000 would have been guard cavalry – again, like their Egyptian counterparts – made up of aristocrats who were obliged to share danger with their king.

1,000 light cavalry, equipped with javelins and swords and probably carrying shields.

10,000 elite phalanx, the *Argyraspides* ('silver shields'), equipped with 21-foot pikes (*sarissae*), backed up by short swords. They were protected by helmets, linen or metal cuirasses and small round shields strapped to the left arm. These troops were of high morale.

25,000 Seleucid/mercenary phalanx, armed and equipped as above. About 80 per cent would have been Seleucid and the remainder mercenary. These troops were of average quality. It has been plausibly suggested that many of them wore trousers beneath their tunics.

5,000 Arab light infantry javelineers, unarmoured and wearing simple tunics and short cloaks.

5,000 Arab light infantry archers, similarly clothed.

8,625 other light infantry javelineers, unarmoured. They would have included Medes and Cilicians.

2,875 other light infantry archers, unarmoured and also including Medes and Cilicians.

102 Indian elephants, crewed by a driver and three armoured men in a tower who carried javelins, pikes and bows.

THE SELEUCID EMPIRE

The Seleucid Empire (312–64 BC) took its name from Seleucus, one of Alexander the Great's leading generals. Seleucus became governor of Babylonia in 321 BC, two years after Alexander's death. He engaged in a prolonged power struggle with others of Alexander's generals who were intent on seizing as many as possible of their leader's conquests for their own enrichment. Seleucus was at first challenged in his Babylonian rule by Antigonus, Alexander's successor in the Macedonian kingdom. With the help of Ptolemy I, however, who had assumed Alexander's mantle in Egypt, Seleucus regained his power in Babylonia and spent 30 years extending his rule east towards the Indus River and west to Syria and Anatolia.

The alliance between Seleucus and the Ptolemys of Egypt soured over time, however, and the enmity came to a head when Ptolemy Ceraunus, son of Ptolemy I, assassinated Seleucus in 281BC. From then on the Seleucid and Ptolemaic dynasties were engaged in a constant struggle for dominance in what is now the Near East.

CANNAE 2 AUGUST 216 BC

The Battle of Cannae was one of the bloodiest in history. According to the Greek historian Polybius, the Romans lost 70,000 men in a single day. Modern scholars have trimmed that figure to 50,000, but have compared the scale of the Roman losses to those sustained by the huge armies on the Western Front during World War I.

BACKGROUND

The battle of Cannae was the third major confrontation in the Second Punic War, itself the second of three protracted wars between Rome and the Carthaginians of North Africa, fought between 264 and 146 BC. Because Carthage was founded by the Phoenicians, a Semitic people from the coast of what is now Lebanon, whom the Romans called *Poeni*, these wars have come to be known as the Punic Wars.

Carthage had built for itself a large trading empire centred on North Africa and the Mediterranean by the fifth century BC. It included the entire North African coast, southern Spain, Corsica, Sardinia and Sicily. Given Roman expansion into the region by the third century BC, it was inevitable that there would be conflict between the two. The First Punic War ran from 264 to 241 BC, and began with a dispute between Rome and Carthage over Sicily. In 264 BC the Carthaginians established a presence on the island, to which the Romans retaliated by sending a fleet to Sicily in 260 BC, which expelled the Carthaginians from Corsica, but failed to gain total control of Sicily. The struggle for control of Sicily

continued until 241 BC when a Roman fleet of 200 warships gave the Romans control of the sea lanes and forced the collapse of the Carthaginian stronghold in Sicily.

Undeterred by these defeats at the hands of the Romans, the Carthaginians continued with expansion in the Mediterranean, when Hamilcar Barca, Hannibal's father, invaded southern Spain in 237 BC and founded a new capital at Cartago Nova (what is now Cartagena). By 219 BC, Hannibal, taking up his father's mantle, had captured the town of Saguntum which, according to a treaty signed between Rome and Carthage immediately after the First Punic War, was a city with which the Romans had 'friendship'. The Romans took this attack as an act of war, and demanded that Hannibal be surrendered to them.

HANNIBAL

Hannibal's response was to take an army of 40,000 troops and march through southern France, across the Alps, and into northern Italy. His strategic aim was to take the war onto Italian soil and fight Rome on its own territory. In the winter of 218 BC he fought his first major battle with Rome at Trebia in northern Italy. Hannibal defeated the Roman forces at Trebia and then progressed into central and southern Italy.

Rather than confront him directly, the Romans evolved a strategy of trying to contain Hannibal, although in 217 BC they were drawn into battle again at Lake Trasimene, in central Italy. Not surprisingly, the Romans were worried. Their losses at Trebia and subsequently at Lake Trasimene shook them deeply. They appointed a dictator, Quintus Fabius Maximus, to take control of the Roman state and army in order to meet the Carthaginian threat. He created a large field army in a short time. Fabius avoided battle with Hannibal whilst following him around Italy, occupying strong positions, earning himself the nickname 'The Delayer'. Fabius' delaying strategy was unpopular with the Romans. It was against Roman ideals of battle, which valued bold moves and open battle. Fabius was recalled to Rome and a new strategy was formed. The largest Roman army ever was assembled with the two consuls of Rome in charge, determined to try to defeat Hannibal in open battle once and for all.

Hannibal was about 31 by the time of the battle of Cannae. He had contracted a severe eye infection after Trebia, which had worsened to the point where he lost the use of the affected eye. His long period of command meant that, although he was still young, he was very experienced. His army had been together for quite a long time on campaign by now and were themselves experienced in fighting as a unit.

Hannibal's cavalry were his most important unit. He often used his light Numidian cavalry to goad the Romans into battle before they were ready, which he had done, for example, at Trebia. The Numidians were some of the best horsemen of the ancient world. They rode without saddles or armour, with a simple rope bridle. At Trebia they positioned themselves just outside the Roman camp and taunted the Romans with insults.

THE ROMAN ARMY

The main unit of the Roman army was the legion. It was made up of five parts:

✝ the light infantry (*velites*): 1,200 men who fought in small groups but for administrative purposes were attached to the maniples. Each man was armed with a bundle of javelins and, at least by the early second century BC, a short stabbing sword (*gladius*), and carried a small circular shield.

✝ the first line of heavy infantry (*hastati*): 1,200 men in ten maniples of 120. These were armed with *pila* (the *pilum* is a heavy javelin designed to penetrate the target's shield and armour), swords, shields, helmets and body armour. These men were the youngest.

✝ the second line of heavy infantry (*principes*): 1,200 men in ten maniples of 120, armed with *pila*, swords, shields, helmets and body armour.

✝ the third line of heavy infantry (*triarii*): 600 men in ten maniples of 60, armed with spears, swords, shields, helmets and body armour. These men were the oldest and most experienced veterans. In all three lines of heavy infantry, the helmet was of bronze and the shield long and cylindrical, constructed of plywood covered with calfskin.

✝ cavalry (*equites*): 300 men in ten troops (*turmae*) of 30, each *turma* commanded by three decurions. Roman cavalry were of fairly poor quality, because there was not a strong cavalry tradition in the Roman army.

Each legion was accompanied by a unit of Latin and Italian allies of about the same size. Such an allied unit was called an *ala* (plural: *alae*) or wing, because it was deployed on the flanks of the legions. The *alae* had a similar internal organisation and tactical system to the legions.

ROMAN TACTICS

The heavy infantry were arranged in three lines, one behind the other: *hastati* in front, *principes* in the middle and *triarii* in the rear. The ten maniples in each line were ranged side by side with spaces between them equal to the width of a maniple. The line behind was staggered to allow its maniples to cover the gaps between the maniples of the line ahead. This was termed the 'quincunx', or checkerboard formation. Each maniple was an independent unit commanded by its senior centurion. At times orders might be given to an entire line to advance or retreat. In most cases a line could only go forwards or backwards. It was very difficult to manoeuvre the entire line, for example, to wheel it to face a new direction; that would have required giving orders to every centurion in charge of a maniple. The legion of thirty maniples was very good at attacking to its front but had difficulty in doing anything else. The cavalry was massed on the flanks and the light infantry either supported them, or were deployed ahead of the main lines.

THE ROMAN COMMANDERS

In accordance with Roman practice, the generals, L. Aemilius Paullus and C. Terentius Varro, were also the consuls of the year. According to Polybius, Paullus was considered by the Senate to be likely to fight well because he had been responsible for a recent successful campaign in Illyria (the modern Balkans). Varro, on the other hand, did not have military experience, and the difference between the two was to prove important. Polybius reports how they disagreed with one another about tactics constantly. This situation was not improved by the fact that, following the rules laid down by the Roman Senate at that time, the two held command on alternate days. In effect, not only was there a war between Rome and Hannibal; there was also a tug-of-war between Paullus and Varro. Fortunately, they were not completely alone with one another: they were assisted by Marcus Atilius and Gnaeus Servilius, who had been the consuls for Rome in the previous year

When the Romans first advanced close to Hannibal's camp, Paullus looked at the terrain and said it was senseless to fight on such flat ground when their enemy had such an advantage in cavalry. His advice was to look for ground where the Roman infantry would be at more of an advantage. Varro completely ignored him the next day, because it was

his turn to be in command, and set the troops straight at the Carthaginians, in an inconclusive engagement.

HANNIBAL'S TACTICS

Hannibal's calculations were that his front line could not keep back the Roman legions. His plan, therefore, was to manipulate the Roman attack onto his front line, hoping he could entice the Romans through any gaps they created as they fought. This was a trap to make the Roman infantry vulnerable to his Libyan infantry. The Numidians would engage the Romans on the right, while the Gallic and Spanish cavalry would break through the Roman cavalry on the left and attack the Romans from behind. Hannibal was planning to trap the Romans by surrounding them.

PRELUDE TO BATTLE

The day after Varro's charge at the Carthaginians, Paullus took command and split his forces, setting up two Roman camps: a main camp on the north-west side of the River Aufidus and a smaller one on the south-east bank of the river. According to Polybius, the Roman troops were clearly pessimistic about their chances of victory. Some had already fought Hannibal, and they were still conscious of their defeats by him. In the days before the battle, therefore, Paullus made a speech to the troops, encouraging them to believe they were in an excellent position. Proving that he had thought a good deal about tactics and about Hannibal's previous victories over Rome, he detailed to the soldiers what he thought had gone wrong at the battles of Trebia and Lake Trasimene, and pointed out how conditions at Cannae were different.

The battle started slowly and continued through several days. For the first three days there were large-scale cavalry skirmishes, not always to Hannibal's advantage. Back in Rome, messengers constantly brought news of the events at Cannae, and the city was at fever pitch. Frantic sacrificing and offerings of prayers

went on continuously in the city's temples, and oracles were consulted on every street corner, so desperate were the Romans to know what was going to happen.

On the day of the main battle, Varro was in command. He drew out the troops from both the Roman camps, and positioned his assembled force on the south-east bank of the River Aufidus, facing inland, with their backs to the Adriatic. He put the Roman cavalry on his right wing, closest to the river, his infantry in the centre and his allied cavalry on the left wing. A screen of lightly armed skirmishers was placed in front of the whole force.

Hannibal brought his full force out and faced his adversaries. On his left, on the river bank, he put his own Iberian and Gallic cavalry, directly opposite the

Roman cavalry. He placed his Numidian cavalry on his left wing, and in the centre were his Iberian, Gallic and Carthaginian heavy infantry. Hannibal did not form his army up in a straight line, unlike the Romans. He created a line that bulged forwards in the middle, so that the whole army was in a rough crescent formation.

THE COURSE OF THE BATTLE

In his account of the battle, Polybius gives us a vivid image of how it may have looked to those taking part. He describes the Gallic troops as naked, that the Iberians wore short tunics with stripes of purple on the edges, and says the whole scene as they advanced was bizarre and terrifying. The sun was rising, but the low rays did not dazzle either army because they faced north and south.

The two armies' skirmishers engaged inconclusively, then the battle began in earnest when the Iberian and Gallic cavalry charged the Roman cavalry. Instead of advancing and retreating, as was the custom, Hannibal's cavalry dismounted when they reached the Roman lines and this part of the battle became a desperate, hand-to-hand slaughter. The dismounting of the cavalry may be explained by an anecdote in Plutarch's account of the battle. He says that the consul Paullus, in charge of the cavalry, was wounded, and so he dismounted his horse. His staff followed him and the rest of the Roman cavalry assumed it was an order, so they dismounted also. Hannibal is supposed to have commented that the Roman cavalry might as well have surrendered themselves in chains. This probably happened during the initial phase of fighting on the Roman right wing.

The Carthaginians hacked their way through and proceeded along the river bank, pursuing the Romans as they went. In the meantime, the Roman infantry had engaged with the Carthaginian centre. As he had planned, Hannibal's Gallic heavy infantry was pushed back by the Romans, but as the Romans pushed through, deeper into the Gallic centre, the Carthaginian heavy infantry closed in on them from both flanks. Both Paullus and Hannibal were in the thick of the fighting themselves, urging their troops forward.

The cavalry on Hannibal's right flank drew the energies of the Roman allied cavalry and prevented it from assisting the Roman infantry, so heavily engaged in the centre. While this was happening, the Carthaginian left flank cavalry, which had driven the Roman cavalry all along the riverbank, regrouped and came hurtling back into the battle, coming up behind the Roman infantry. Hannibal's trap was sprung: the Romans were surrounded.

As Polybius tells us, the Romans could continue to fight while they were able to maintain a single front line, which they could turn in different directions as the enemy attacked. Once they were fighting in several fronts at the same time, however, the outer lines of the circle were cut down. Then the circle grew smaller and smaller as the Romans were butchered where they stood. Some Romans did escape, but not many. Perhaps only 70 cavalry, out of 6,000, survived. The Roman historian Livy gives a different account of how the Carthaginians defeated Rome. According to him, approximately 500 Carthaginian cavalry, armed with spears and shields, rode over early in the battle to the Roman lines, threw their arms on the ground and surrendered. The Romans passed them through to the rear lines of the battle, where they remained for some time, apparently completely uninvolved in the fight. Once the battle had reached its peak, however, these Carthaginians rose up and, seizing weapons from among the hundreds that lay by that time on the battlefield, savagely attacked the Romans from the rear.

THE TACTICAL LEGACY

Modern military historians have described Hannibal's tactics at Cannae as 'the double envelopment', and continue to study them up to the present day. Most recently, the US General Norman Schwarzkopf has claimed that his strategies in the first Gulf War were also inspired by Hannibal's example.

AFTERMATH

According to Livy, the Romans lost 48,200 men: 45,000 infantry and 2,700 cavalry, and 4,500 were captured. The figures seem more plausible than those quoted by Polybius. Certainly more than half of the Roman army was destroyed, but the cost for the Carthaginians was also high: estimates of their losses range from 5,700 to 8,000.

TROOPS AT CANNAE

THE ROMAN ARMY – TOTAL 76,000

Roman legions – 7 legions of 5,000 infantry each, a total of 35,000 men. 10,262 of these were light infantry skirmishers (*velites*). The rest (24,730) were heavy infantry.

Roman cavalry – 2,400
Allied heavy infantry – 24,730
Allied light infantry skirmishers – 10,262
Allied cavalry – 3,600

The Romans in fact had 86,000 troops in total but they left one Roman legion plus one allied legion – 10,000 men in total – behind to guard the Roman camp.

THE CARTHAGINIAN ARMY – TOTAL 50,000

Libyan heavy infantry – 8,000
Spanish heavy infantry – 4,000
Gallic heavy infantry – 20,000
Numidian light cavalry – 3,000
Spanish heavy cavalry – 3,000
Gallic heavy cavalry – 4,000
Lightly armed spear-bearers (skirmishers) – 6,000
Balearic slingers (skirmishers) – 2,000

Varro escaped but Paullus was killed, as were several other high-ranking Roman officials. Between a quarter and a third of Rome's senators were killed or captured at Cannae. Both Livy and Polybius testify to the profound shock felt by the Romans that so many of their important public figures had died in one single battle. Over 50,000 men lay dead or dying in an area of not much more than a few square kilometres. Cannae was a stunning blow to the Romans: the largest army they had ever fielded had been annihilated. Livy describes horrible mutilations among the dead, and even tells us that, after the battle, men left wounded on the field dug holes in the earth for themselves, inserted their heads and covered themselves with earth in the hope of suffocating.

Despite his victory, Hannibal did not do what even a modern observer would expect him to have done: he did not march on Rome. Livy notes this, calling Cannae less grave for its long-term results than for the immediate death toll. Hannibal was urged to march on Rome by his fellow commanders, one of whom, according to legend, said, 'Hannibal, although you are the world's greatest commander, you do not know how to use your victories.' No one knows why Hannibal did not follow through on his triumphs.

The Romans were horrified when news reached them of the defeat and its scale. First reports apparently made no mention of survivors. Rome was told the entire force had simply been wiped out. According to the Roman orator Cicero, however, once the Romans had a fuller picture, and Hannibal asked for ransoms for the Roman soldiers he had captured, the Senate refused to pay any ransoms. Their reported attitude was that soldiers were supposed either to die or to be victorious: those who did neither were simply not worth noticing, let alone ransoming. This attitude, Cicero says, broke Hannibal's spirit: he could not understand an enemy that threw its troops away when it most needed them.

Rome finally defeated the Carthaginians 14 years later at the Battle of Zama in 202 BC. The Carthaginian army was overwhelmed and, since Carthage did not have the resources or the will to continue fighting, the Second Punic War was over.

Hannibal survived Zama and helped to revive Carthage's prosperity, but political rivalry eventually forced him into exile and he became a mercenary commander fighting for the Hellenistic kingdoms of the East, especially those hostile to Rome. Hunted down by Roman agents, he took his own life in Bithynia in 183 BC.

CAVALRY IN BATTLE

A striking feature of Hannibal's use of different kinds of troops in battle is his skilful deployment of cavalry. Yet it needs to be remembered that mounted troops had been an element of warfare for only about 200 years.

The earliest use of horses in warfare was as the motive power for chariots carrying archers and drivers, in cultures such as the Hittite and Egyptian empires that clashed at the battle of Qadesh in 1275 BC. The horse itself had not been domesticated until some date between 3000 and 2500 BC; learning how to breed horses strong enough to carry heavily armed riders at speed took centuries. It was not until the emergence of distinct military tactics for mounted troops that true cavalry can be said to have evolved. This occurred among the Scythians of the Near East, who clashed with the forces of the Persian king Darius I when he invaded Scythia in 512 BC. The Scythians were very skilful riders, heavily armed with bows, short swords, war axes and spears, and carrying shields to protect themselves. The Persians employed cavalry extensively in their campaigns against the Greeks and developed body armour for cavalrymen. Philip of Macedon expanded the cavalryman's armoury with the 10-foot spear or sarissa, which gave its user a longer reach in combat, and achieved significant victories against Persian cavalry armed with shorter javelins at battles such as that of the River Granicus in 334 BC.

Cannae marked a significant departure from the arming of previous cavalry formations, in that the cavalry on both sides carried shields. Cavalry often performed the function of advancing towards the enemy, attacking them with a shower of javelins thrown from horseback and then withdrawing. Hannibal employed this tactic at all his battles. Armed with shields and short swords, however, both Hannibal's and the Roman cavalry were able to descend from their horses and fight on foot, as we are told happened at Cannae. Hannibal also exploited the mobility of his cavalry by having them attack at unexpected moments. At Trebia he had concealed about 2,000 cavalry in a gully adjacent to the battlefield and brought them into the battle at a point when their freshness and speed of movement had an enormous impact on the battle-weary Romans. His technique at Cannae was similar: he allowed the cavalry under Hasdrubal to engage the Roman cavalry, drive it back, withdraw and regroup, so that they could then attack the Roman rear in a much fresher condition than infantry who had slogged their way all through the battle.

SILARUS RIVER 70 BC

BACKGROUND

Roman victories in war and a constant struggle against piracy in the third and second centuries BC had filled Italy with a huge and dangerous horde of Roman captives who, as was usual in the ancient world, had been made into slaves. It has been estimated that slaves may have constituted as much as a third of the population. The Roman economy was based on agriculture and the large farm estates of this period relied heavily on slave labour. Slaves had few human rights in the Roman world: they were mere property.

There had already been violent slave rebellions in Sicily in 139 and 104 BC. According to the Greek historian Plutarch, the gladiators, led by Spartacus, who broke out of a gladiatorial school at Capua in the summer of 73 BC, were responding to the fact that they were compelled to fight as gladiators for no better reason than that their owners unjustly insisted on it. They had committed no crimes to merit such a life. Their aim, therefore, was simply to be free of a fate forced on them by the unscrupulousness of others.

In fact, Spartacus' escape was part of a larger plan to free 200 slaves. Once out of the gladiatorial school, he and his fellow gladiators armed themselves with weapons intended for other gladiators that they found in wagons nearby. Soon they were joined by other slaves and people with little to lose such as shepherds. The rebel army spent two years marching through the Italian peninsula, mainly in the south, defeating Roman forces of various sizes and capabilities. At first the Romans did not seem to take the threat very seriously. According to the Roman historian Appian, they looked on Spartacus' force as nothing more than bandits. Eventually, however, they became more concerned and, after a series of commanders and their armies had been defeated, appointed M. Lincinius Crassus praetor, with eight legions under his command to deal with this threat.

GLADIATORIAL GAMES

Gladiatorial games were becoming more frequent and popular during this period, though they had not yet reached the excesses of the Imperial period. The games originated in the fourth century BC in Campania, the area around Capua, where gladiators were trained and housed. Most of the gladiators were slaves, but some were free men. The school that Spartacus and his fellow gladiators broke out of was a private one.

SPARTACUS

Spartacus came from Thrace, and was a slave trained as a gladiator. According to Appian, Spartacus had also fought in the Roman army. Plutarch describes him as being more noble than the ignominious end he was to meet, and that he had many Greek qualities. Whatever Spartacus' experiences might have been, it seems likely he had first-hand knowledge of the Roman army.

THE SLAVE ARMY

One of the great weaknesses of Spartacus' army was that it was a mixed group of slaves from everywhere Rome had fought wars; it included large numbers of Thracians, Germans and Gauls and smaller numbers of Spaniards and Numidians. It would inevitably have been difficult to maintain discipline and unity of purpose in a force in which so many languages and cultures had been brought together.

When the revolt began, Spartacus' fellow rebels were all gladiators, but the force quickly expanded as it was joined by rural slaves, herdsmen and shepherds. It appears that, although the rebels had the military advantage for much of the period of their freedom, they had no particular aim other than to remain free. In the circumstances, this was inevitable. Escape from a gladiatorial school had no development: there was no one to whom the gladiators could appeal for a change in their lives. Spartacus probably could do no more than react to the immediate danger of annihilation by the Roman legions.

The army itself was, however, well organised and efficient in obtaining the weapons and other supplies it needed to continue fighting. Appian records that, by the third year of the uprising, Spartacus occupied the region around Thurii, in the 'instep' of Italy. Spartacus forbade the import of gold or silver there, and would only allow copper and iron to be brought in. This ensured the insurgents had plenty of material for repairing damaged weapons and making new ones.

It was clear that there was a lack of unity among those who followed Spartacus, however. He led his army to northern Italy in the hope that it would disperse, the slaves making for their homes in Gaul and Thrace. Yet they did not. Plutarch implies this was because they preferred a life of pillaging in Italy.

THE ROMAN ARMY OF THE LATE REPUBLIC

The main unit of the Roman army continued to be the legion. It was still recruited from citizens, but eligibility was no longer connected with property, and most legionaries of this period were volunteers drawn from the poorest citizenry, attracted by adequate wages and the prospect of promotion. Because men no longer bought their own equipment, property distinctions lost the importance they had once had and all legionaries were equipped in the same way: as heavy infantrymen armed with a short spear, sword, body-shield, helmet and cuirass.

In 88 BC most of Italy was granted Roman citizenship. Consequently the allied wings (*alae*) that had figured prominently in earlier Roman armies virtually disappeared, and Italians simply joined the legions as Roman citizens.

The maniple was replaced, as the basic tactical unit, by the cohort, consisting of three maniples combined and numbering 480 men. For administrative purposes each cohort was divided into six centuries, each century commanded by a centurion. The most senior centurion commanded the entire cohort. The professional legion of this period consisted of ten cohorts, equal in size and uniformly equipped; thus a legion at full strength had 4,800 men. The legion continued to be led by six tribunes, but it became increasingly common for one of the army commander's senior subordinates, or legates, to be the commander of a legion.

TACTICS

The cohort legion was far more flexible than the manipular legion. It normally had a single commander who had to issue orders to, and direct, ten cohort commanders, whereas in the manipular legion a pair of tribunes with equal authority had to pass their instructions on to 30 maniple commanders. Because all the cohorts were identical in size and equipment, they no longer needed to have a fixed position in the line; nor did the legion itself have to deploy in three lines, but could adapt to the particular situation. Three lines were still common in the late Republic, with four cohorts in the first line and three each in the second and third, but we also hear of legions formed in two lines of cohorts, or four. A single line of cohorts was dangerously brittle and was used only in desperate situations. Cohorts were also more suited than the smaller maniples to detached duty.

Well trained and led, the legionaries of this period proved capable of taking on and beating almost any opposition. They consistently defeated far more numerous opponents. Roman infantry tactics were very aggressive.

CRASSUS

M. Licinius Crassus was in his early forties at the time of the Spartacan revolt. One of the wealthiest men in late Republican Rome, he was the city's greatest landlord. He did his best to increase his personal fortune by all kinds of investments and shady deals, but his primary concern was extending his political influence. His driving ambition was military glory: he took on the command against Spartacus when many other Romans were reluctant to do so. Because of the total humiliation that would have followed from it, a defeat at the hands of a slave army would have been a major blow to any political career.

PRELUDE TO BATTLE

After Spartacus' force had defeated local Roman troops, Publius Varinius was appointed as Roman commander. Two subordinate commanders, Furius and L. Cossinius, separately engaged the rebels and lost, Cossinius first narrowly escaping capture, and then dying in battle with the insurgents. Varinius too

suffered defeats: most ignominiously, his very horse was captured.

Rome now began to take the revolt more seriously and in 72 BC L. Gellius Publicola and Gn. Cornelius Lentulus, the consuls for the year, were sent out against Spartacus. The military tide was swelling in Rome's favour but the advantage still lay with the rebels. Spartacus led his men north, planning to escape from Italy over the Alps, and for the slaves to return to their homelands. On the way he defeated both the consuls and C. Cassius Longinus, the governor of Cisalpine Gaul; the consuls were recalled to Rome in disgrace.

Rome then cast around for other means to defeat Spartacus. M. Licinius Crassus was given command by the Senate of eight legions, six of which were newly raised, to attack Spartacus. Crassus ordered his subordinate Mummius to follow Spartacus' army but not engage it. Mummius ignored the order and attacked. His two legions were defeated, and reportedly a large number of them ran away from the battlefield.

Crassus notably revived an ancient form of punishment at this point. He inflicted the fate of decimation on the members of Mummius' legions who survived. He selected 500 soldiers who had run from the battle, then divided them into 50 groups of 10. Each group of 10 had to select a victim by lot from among them. Then the remaining nine were ordered to beat the tenth man to death, while the rest of the army looked on.

Having displayed his will to succeed, Crassus moved to face Spartacus, whose army had refused to disband and disperse across the Alps. Spartacus retreated to the sea, making for Sicily, where slave revolts had taken place in the past. He negotiated with the Sicilian pirates and arranged a crossing by means of which he hoped to land 2,000 men in Sicily to fan the flames of revolt there. The pirates, however,

TROOPS AT SILARUS RIVER

ROMAN ARMY – TOTAL 44,000
Legionary cohorts – 38,000
Skirmishers (archers and javelineers) – 2,000
Auxiliary heavy cavalry – 3,000
Auxiliary light cavalry, Numidian – 1,000

THE SLAVES – TOTAL APPROXIMATELY 70,000
Gladiator-style heavy infantry – 7,000
Roman-style heavy infantry – 22,000
Rabble/Italian peasants – 24,000
Tribal warriors/infantry – 10,000
Skirmishers (archers and javelineers) – 5,000
Light cavalry – 1,000
Heavy cavalry – 700

These figures, particularly for the slave army, are estimates.

reneged on their agreement and failed to turn up with ships at the appointed time.

In the winter of 72–71 BC, the rebel forces were trapped at Rhegium, in the peninsula of Bruttium. Despite its being a huge undertaking, Crassus built a 35-mile earthwork, 15 feet high and wide, all the way across the isthmus at Rhegium, and bottled up Spartacus' army. The insurgents were completely isolated.

Plutarch tells us that in the middle of the winter, Spartacus succeeded in filling in one part of the ditch with earth, tree branches and other pieces of wood, and managed to lead one third of his army out from behind Crassus' blockade. Crassus saw what was happening, and pursued a part of the force that had deliberately separated itself from Spartacus and attacked it, but Spartacus appeared, rallied his men and defeated Crassus. Spartacus' force may have been splintering at this point, because Plutarch tells us Crassus then pursued two other forces that had separated themselves from Spartacus, attacked them and defeated them decisively. Spartacus then made for the mountains of Petelia.

A Roman force pursued him, but he defeated them. According to Plutarch, this victory went to the heads of Spartacus' army, and they no longer obeyed the orders they were given.

Crassus wrote to the Senate demanding the return of the legions from Macedonia which M. Licinius Lucullus had been ordered to bring back to deal with the revolt, but he became impatient, thinking Lucullus might snatch his fame away.

After several further battles, Spartacus turned to face Crassus for the decisive encounter, either in desperation, as Appian says, or out of over-confidence, in the opinion of Plutarch. This was exactly what Crassus wanted. He was keen to deal with the slaves once and for all before his rivals Pompey and Lucullus came to steal his glory. The final battle was fought at the head of the River Silarus in northwestern Lucania. Plutarch tells us that Spartacus killed his horse before the battle in a defiant gesture to his troops to raise their morale. Very little is known of the course of the battle, except that the slaves were utterly defeated and Spartacus was killed.

AFTERMATH

Spartacus' slave army fell apart after the battle. In an orgy of retaliation and savage punishment, the Romans crucified 6,000 captured slaves along the Appian Way, the main road from Rome to Capua, as a way of saying to every slave in Roman territory, 'See what happens when you rebel'. Crassus was rewarded with the honour of a public ovation. Five thousand of the slaves escaped and fled north, where they were defeated by Pompey, on the march with his legions back to Italy. This gave Pompey the opportunity to claim that while Crassus had won the battle, he had finished the war.

Spartacus' name was chosen by the German revolutionary socialist group of 1914–18, the Spartacus League, to symbolize their aims of social justice.

Some of the historical sources that mention Spartacus suggest that he may have served in the Roman army. All are agreed, however, that he was a slave. He is also described as a man of unusual qualities: competent and humane, he is called 'more Greek than Thracian'. His rebellion began when he and about seventy other gladiators escaped from a privately owned gladiatorial school in Capua, just north of what is now Naples, in 73 BC. One source says that Spartacus' wife was with him when he was enslaved and that she was part of the rebellion.

The group took refuge on the slopes of nearby Mount Vesuvius, where they were joined by other runaway slaves. At first, Roman military response to the rebellion was tentative: an initial force of 4,000 sent against Spartacus was easily defeated, and their weapons provided Spartacus' force with a welcome addition to their armoury.

Over the next year, however, as the rebels came to dominate much of southern Italy, and their numbers are said to have grown to about 90,000, several larger Roman forces were sent out to quell the revolt, but without success. The two consuls for the year 72 led four legions against Spartacus and might have defeated him but for the fact that Spartacus led his army north towards the Alps with the intention of allowing them to disperse out of Italy. The rebel group, however, refused to disband, and Spartacus then led them south again, hoping to cross over into Sicily. By this time eight legions had been raised and, led by their commander Marcus Licinius Crassus, bottled up the rebels in the peninsula of Bruttium (in the 'toe' of Italy). Spartacus' army divided. The Gauls and Germans were defeated, then Spartacus himself was killed in a second battle.

GLADIATORS

The word gladiator is derived from *gladius*, the Latin name for the Roman short sword. The Romans claimed that they based the practice of gladiatorial combat on the example of the Etruscans, who, they said, included such combats in their funeral games. The earliest recorded example in Roman history, in the third century BC, does seem to have been part of funeral games. From then on the practice seems to have gained popularity until it became a major preoccupation of Roman society. When the emperor Trajan held his triumph in AD 107, as many as 5,000 gladiators are reported to have taken part. Amphitheatres survive in many parts of the Roman Empire, testifying to the popularity of the practice far beyond Rome itself.

The ranks of gladiators were carefully graded and classified. The core gladiatorial scenario was a fight to the death between two individuals, so the basic gladiatorial fighting unit was the pair. Samnites fought with large shields, short swords and plumed helmets; Thracians, armed with round shields and curved-bladed daggers, were often paired with *mirmillones*, armed with helmets, shields and swords. Another common pairing pitted a gladiator armed only with a net and trident (*retiarius*) against a fully armed opponent called the pursuer (*secutor*). Other gladiatorial 'types' were *andabatae*, *dimachaeri*, who fought with two knives, and *essedarii* (chariot fighters).

Most gladiators were slaves, or in some cases criminals who had been given a choice between punishment and fighting in gladiatorial combat. It was possible for a private citizen to become a gladiator, but he had to take an oath that he accepted the vicissitudes of the gladiatorial life. It may seem a poor bargain, but gladiators received three meals a day and had their own sleeping quarters, and did have the chance to win prizes.

TIGRANOCERTA
69 BC

BACKGROUND

Lying in the area that we now call eastern Turkey, the region the Romans referred to as Armenia was a high plateau with steep mountain ranges. Until c. 92 BC it was a patchwork of states owing allegiance to different rulers, but around that time King Tigranes began to acquire control of much of the surrounding territory. Tigranes had spent part of his early life as a hostage in the court of the Parthian king Mithradates II, and acquired his freedom by ceding to him land in what is now northwestern Iran. Once established in his own territory, Tigranes made war against the Parthians and Medes, annexed northern Mesopotamia and, in 83 BC, accepted the crown offered him by Syria. Tigranes then took the title 'king of kings' and started building a new capital for himself, the fortress of Tigranocerta. According to Plutarch it was a rich and beautiful city.

Rome's relationship with the region it called Pontus (what is now northern Turkey and the shores of the Black Sea) had been a constant struggle for domination. In 88 BC, Mithradates of Pontus had made a determined effort to conquer much of Asia Minor and the Aegean, but was soundly defeated at Chaeronea and Orchomenos by Sulla, dictator of Rome in 82–79 BC. By 75 BC, however, Mithradates felt in a sufficiently strong position to try to regain some of his former conquests, and invaded Bithynia (now western Turkey), a province that had been ceded

to Rome on the death of its monarch. L. Licinius Lucullus, who had fought against Mithradates under Sulla, had been given command of Cilicia and Asia during his consulship in 74 BC, and it now fell to him to fight Mithradates once more. After being defeated by Lucullus at Cabira in 73 BC, Mithradates fled and sought protection from Lucullus' armies with his son-in-law Tigranes.

By the end of the year 70 BC, all of Asia Minor was again under Rome's control and the Mithradatic war seemed over. But Lucullus, determined to subdue Mithradates once and for all, pressed the Armenians to surrender him. In 69 BC, although he probably did not have the support of the Roman senate, he led an army of no more than 16,000 infantry, with 3,000 cavalry and some slingers and archers across the Euphrates and invaded Armenia.

L. LICINIUS LUCULLUS

During the years 73–68 BC he was responsible for many hard-won victories in the Near East for which the Roman general Pompey would later take credit when he was appointed triumvir. But Lucullus did not suffer all that badly: he made himself very rich through his Eastern campaigns, and on his return to Rome became renowned for his incredibly lavish lifestyle, houses and gardens.

expectations, boastings, and barbaric threatenings.' With hindsight we understand what disciplined and determined fighters the Roman legions were, but Tigranes had not previously fought the Romans and did not have that foreknowledge. In the past, Eastern armies had very successfully relied on overwhelming numbers to defeat an enemy. When he saw the Romans approaching, Tigranes famously remarked that they were 'too few to be an army, too many to be an embassy' and said he was sorry he had only one Roman general to fight.

THE ROMAN ARMY

The main unit of the Roman army continued to be the legion. It was still recruited from citizens, but whereas in the past men bought their own equipment, now legionnaires were all equipped in the same way. The majority of legionnaires were volunteers from the poorest citizens and the army provided them with a living wage. Thus the old property distinctions which had formerly been of such importance no longer mattered.

In 88 BC most of Italy was granted Roman citizenship. Consequently the allied wings (*alae*) that had figured prominently in earlier Roman armies virtually disappeared, and Italians simply joined the legions as Roman citizens.

The cohort became the basic tactical unit, replacing the maniple. The cohort was made up of three maniples combined into one unit and numbered approximately 480 men. For administrative purposes each cohort was divided into six centuries, and each century was commanded by a centurion. The most senior centurion commanded the entire cohort. The professional legion of this period consisted of ten cohorts, equal in size and uniformly equipped; thus a legion at full strength had 4,800 men. The legion continued to be led by six tribunes, but it became increasingly common for one of the army commander's senior subordinates, or legates, to be the commander of a legion.

TIGRANES THE GREAT

As he had shown when he freed himself from the condition of a hostage at the court of Mithradates, King Tigranes II, or Tigranes the Great, was a shrewd political operator – as he needed to be to survive as a Near Eastern king – but had little experience as a military leader. Plutarch relates that Tigranes was extremely confident before his battle with Lucullus, especially because military support for his confrontation with Rome was arriving from all sides: forces of Armenians and Gordyenians, Medes and Adiabenians, accompanied by their respective kings, and many Arabians, Albanians and Iberians. As Plutarch puts it, 'All the king's feasts and councils rang of nothing but

TACTICS

The cohort legion was far more flexible than the manipular legion. It normally had a single commander who had to issue orders to, and direct, ten cohort commanders, whereas in the manipular legion a pair of tribunes with equal authority had to pass their instructions on to 30 maniple commanders. Because all the cohorts were identical in size and equipment, they no longer needed to have a fixed position in the line; nor did the legion itself have to deploy in three lines, but could adapt to the particular situation. Three lines were still common in the late Republic, with four cohorts in the first line and three each in the second and third, but we also hear of legions formed in two lines of cohorts, or four. A single line of cohorts was dangerously brittle and was used only in desperate situations. Cohorts were also more suited than the smaller maniples to detached duty.

THE ARMENIAN ARMY

Tigranes' army was huge, but its quality was mostly inferior. Many of the soldiers had been unwillingly pressed into service and lacked the ferocious determination of the Roman legionaries. Compared to the Romans, many of Tigranes' men were badly equipped and poorly trained. The Armenians, like many of their neighbours, relied more on the numbers of their troops than on their quality.

The Cataphracts, wearing chain mail and carrying long, heavy spears, were the most daunting of Tigranes' troops. There were also many archers in Tigranes' army. Most of them were probably not very skilful, but the Romans had not faced so many archers in battle before. They had few archers of their own and, if there had been a prolonged archery battle, the Romans would have lost.

THE SITE OF THE BATTLE

The site of the city of Tigranocerta is uncertain. We know it was on the borders of Armenia and Cappadocia, so it was probably roughly in the region of what is now northern Syria. The battle was not fought at the city itself but presumably in the area around it. Plutarch describes the battlefield as on a plain with a deep river running through it. There was a ford, to the west of which the Roman army was deployed. The Armenians were positioned on the eastern side of the river, while the Romans started on the western side. There was also a hill with easy slopes and a flat plain on top, on the eastern side of the river, where the Armenian cavalry, the right flank of their army, were positioned. It was about four furlongs (about 800 metres), or four *stadia* by Roman measurement, from where the Romans forded the river.

PRELUDE TO BATTLE

When Lucullus entered Armenia he engaged in some skirmishes with small deployments of the Armenian army, which he won. Tigranes himself withdrew from Tigranocerta to the armed citadel of Taurus. Lucullus marched directly to Tigranocerta and besieged it, hoping to provoke Tigranes into open battle to defend his capital. Tigranes used some of his best cavalry to break through the Roman siege lines and rescue his concubines from Tigranocerta.

His advisers, among them Mithradates, urged him to avoid pitched battle with the Romans, but he ignored them. Many allies had joined the Armenian army, and Tigranes was keen to fight before Mithradates joined him, because he did not want to share the glory of what he believed would be an overwhelming defeat for the Romans. When the Armenians took the field for battle, Lucullus left 6,000 infantry to carry on the siege of Tigranocerta and led 10,000 infantry (21 cohorts), with all his cavalry, slingers and archers into battle.

Roman Siege Warfare

Siege warfare was a common tactic of war in the ancient world, from the famous Homeric siege of Troy to less familiar but strategically highly important sieges such as Julius Caesar's siege of Alesia in 52 BC, or the siege of Masada in AD 73–74. The Roman army was uniquely adapted to success in siege warfare because it possessed engineering knowledge and a concept of logistics.

The Roman army's ability to dig was at least as great as its ability to fight. In the ancient world it was unique in the discipline and foresight which dictated that every Roman military force on the move, however large or small, dug itself a fortified camp every night. Earthworks were thrown up within which the force could bed down, secure in the knowledge that it was defended from attack. Such camps could be expanded at will: fresh earthworks could be thrown up and gatehouses and moats constructed. Many towns and cities throughout the Roman Empire were first built in this fashion.

Besides the security they offered and their potential for being expanded into more permanent bases, overnight forts offered a further, huge advantage: they were supply staging posts. As any army moves into enemy territory, its lines of supply are further and further extended.

A poor general neglects such considerations and suddenly finds himself thousands of miles from home with a starving army that has no fresh supplies of weapons or horses. The Roman camps solved this problem at a stroke: as the Roman army marched, it left behind it a series of fortified posts to defend its lines of supply.

An army that can combine the construction of fortifications with a constant supply of resources is uniquely equipped for siege warfare, as the Roman army proved time and time again. When Lucullus' army advanced into Asia they created their own supply lines; once they reached Tigranocerta, they threw up fortifications that both protected themselves and isolated Tigranocerta from fresh supplies of food. An instance of Roman skill in siege warfare is that their earthworks completely surrounded the cities they besieged; they did not limit themselves to principal roads and access points.

Lucullus' skill in this situation is also demonstrated by his ability to use the forces at his disposal judiciously. Plutarch tells us that some urged Lucullus to abandon his siege and use all his forces to defeat Tigranes' army; others advised the opposite. Lucullus did both: he divided his forces, maintained the siege, defeated Tigranes' army and captured Tigranocerta.

cataphracts

Cataphracts were the heavy cavalry deployed against the Romans in many battles in the Near East, for example at Carrhae in 53 BC, and at Tigranocerta. Their modern name comes from the word the ancient Greeks used to describe them, *kataphraktoi*, meaning 'covered over'. The Romans called them *clibanarii*, 'oven men'. Both names bear witness to the very extensive covering of these troops and even their horses. The Romans called them 'oven men' because they were astonished that anyone could fight in a climate as hot as the Near East's when completely covered not by cloth but by scale-mail, which the Romans called *lorica squamata*. The individual bronze scales used in the scale-mail, measuring roughly 20mm by 12mm, were fitted together to make a garment that covered the chest and back. Cataphracts also wore metal helmets with scale- or chain-mail neck protectors (aventails) and solid metal face-masks. Their arms and legs were sheathed in segmented body armour, of the kind developed by the Persian armies of Darius and Cyrus, with chain mail protecting flexible joints such as the backs of the knees.

The cataphracts' appearance must have been daunting: a totally armoured man without even a face to make him seem human. The cataphract's horse was no less heavily protected. Bronze and iron horse-body armour of the period has been found by archaeologists at Dura Europos, the ruined ancient city in the Syrian desert. Bronze was preferred because iron was rusted by the horse's sweat. The neck and head were protected by separate pieces of armour, so that the horse could move them without difficulty.

The cataphract's main offensive weapon was a spear 3.5m long, which the Greeks called a *kontos*, or bargepole. Cataphracts often held the spear in both hands, but it might also be tied to the horse's saddle, to allow the horse to absorb the shock of impact as the cataphracts crashed into their enemies.

Horses that could carry not only protective armour but also a man similarly clothed had to be large and strong. Such horses were being bred in the Near East by the Persians and the Sarmatians by the end of the first millennium BC. The Parthians, those masters of horse riding, trained their horses to run with a fast, high-stepping action that carried the rider very smoothly, which was especially important for a rider wearing armour. The Parthian way of training horses to run in this manner, which is not instinctive to horses, was to exercise them in ploughed fields, so that the horse was forced to learn to pick up its hooves very quickly to jump over the furrows.

TROOPS AT TIGRANOCERTA

THE ROMANS – TOTAL 17,000
Infantry (Roman legionaries) – 10,000
Cavalry – 5,000
Archers – 1,000
Slingers – 1,000

It should be remembered that Lucullus had left 6,000 legionaries behind to continue the siege of the city of Tigranocerta itself.

THE ARMENIANS – TOTAL 260,000
Archers and slingers – 20,000
Cavalry – 38,000
Cataphracts – 17,000
Heavily armed infantry – 150,000
Engineers – 35,000

These figures are taken from Plutarch's *Life of Lucullus*.

THE **COURSE OF THE BATTLE**

Plutarch tells us that Lucullus attacked confidently and, although vastly outnumbered, achieved a swift victory. He noticed that Tigranes had put the most important part of his army, a troop of cataphracts, in an unsupported position on his right flank. Lucullus swung in upon the cataphracts and drove them into the Armenian centre, in a movement similar to that employed by King Eumenes when he won the battle of Magnesia in 190 BC. The Armenian infantry at once broke into disorder and were pursued and overcome.

Lucullus began the battle by leading his army in haste along the path of the river westward, towards a good ford. The Armenians, seeing the Romans move rapidly away from them, thought they were fleeing; so that when the Roman army swung around and crossed the river, displaying their eagles, armour and weapons lit by the sun, the Armenians were caught unawares. In great confusion the army tried to organize itself. Tigranes kept the main body of the army for himself, while the left wing was commanded by the king of the Adiabenians and the right by the king of the Medes. Most of the heavy-armed cavalry was posted in front of the right flank.

The Romans crossed the river, with Lucullus at their head. When Lucullus saw that the cataphracts were drawn up under a large hill with a broad and open plain on top, he commanded his Thracian and Galatian horse to fall upon their flank and cut with their swords against the Armenian horsemen's lances. At this point, the Romans were attacking the right flank of the Armenian army. Lucullus himself made for the top of the hill with two cohorts of infantry (just under 1,000 men). When they reached it, Lucullus declared, 'We have overcome!' They then marched against the cataphracts and engaged in hand-to-hand combat rather than throwing their javelins, Lucullus calculating that the only vulnerable points on such heavily armed men were their legs, which were best attacked with swords. With great noise and confusion the cataphracts lost their nerve and threw themselves back on their own infantry, whose ranks dissolved.

Once the cataphracts were defeated, the rest of Tigranes' army simply panicked and ran for their lives. With 10,000 Roman legionaries in pursuit, the result was never going to be anything but carnage. Plutarch observes that the Armenians were packed so closely together, because of their huge numbers, that slaughter was inevitable.

AFTERMATH

Tigranes fled the field with some of his men, giving his crown to his son, who in turn gave it to one of his most trusted servants. The servant and the crown were captured by the Romans. Tigranes escaped and was joined by Mithradates in the heart of Armenia.

Lucullus attempted to pursue Tigranes, but the war had the possibility of becoming endless; the further east he went, the more Lucullus risked initiating another war, with the Parthians. Exhausted by their campaign, his troops mutinied; the Roman army in Armenia became a byword for an indisciplined mob. Mithradates, seizing his chance, gathered another army and reoccupied Pontus, while Tigranes reoccupied Cappadocia.

Lucullus was given a triumph in Rome in 63 BC, after which he retired from military service.

Plutarch records that, before Lucullus defeated Tigranes in battle, his forces had a number of skirmishes with parts of Tigranes' army, with the aim of ensuring that soldiers loyal to Tigranes would not be able to reach Tigranocerta and reinforce it against attack. Lucullus' lieutenants Murena and Sextilius destroyed a force of Arabs making their way to defend Tigranocerta, and also trapped Tigranes in a narrow pass, forcing him to abandon all his baggage in order to escape capture.

Lucullus then advanced with all his forces to Tigranocerta and laid siege to it. The city was full of captives from Tigranes' wars of conquest: Greeks captured in Cilicia (modern-day southern Turkey), Adiabenians (from what is now northern Iraq), Assyrians and Cappadocians. Tigranes had destroyed their cities and forced them to move to his own capital. Tigranocerta is said to have been a beautiful city, in which everyone, from the highest to the lowest, wanted to join in the work of making it even more beautiful. Lucullus,

therefore, was convinced that besieging it would draw Tigranes back to defend it, and he would then have the king at his mercy.

Once Lucullus had defeated Tigranes, the Greek captives in Tigranocerta helped him to break the siege of the city and enter it. There was a general plunder of the city, Lucullus and his soldiers helping themselves to what were evidently large amounts of money. Lucullus, an astute man, not only allowed his troops to plunder the city but shared out among them equal portions of part of what he himself had looted. Plutarch tells us that there were in Tigranocerta many players and performers whom Tigranes had invited for the celebrations surrounding the opening of the theatre. Lucullus seized the chance to use these players to celebrate his own triumph of conquering Tigranocerta and its creator. In another example of farsightedness, Lucullus made money available for the many captives still in the city to travel back to their own countries.

BIBRACTE 58 BC

BACKGROUND: GAUL

The battle of Bibracte took place in what is now central France, but in Roman times was part of *Gallia*, or Gaul. The whole of the region the Romans called Gaul covered present-day France, Belgium, Luxembourg and Germany west of the Rhône, an area of over 300,000 square miles, occupied by many Celtic tribes. In the Roman view, however, a more simplified picture emerges. As Julius Caesar famously wrote in the opening lines of his *Commentarii de bello Gallico* (*Commentary on the war in Gaul*), 'all of Gaul is divided into three parts, one of which the Belgae inhabit, the Aquitani the second, and those who in their own language are called Celts, [and] in our [language] Gauls, inhabit the third. All these differ from each other in language, customs and laws.'

Relations between the Gauls and the Romans had been intermittently hostile since the fourth century BC, when tribes from Gaul had migrated into what is now northern Italy and established themselves in permanent settlements. In 390 BC, in an effort to claim northern Italy as their territory, a force of Gauls swept southwards, besieged Rome itself for seven months and left it in ruins after forcing the Roman people to pay a ransom to have them withdraw.

Such an overwhelming defeat left a deep scar on the collective Roman memory. Ever after, the Romans feared another humiliation at the hands of those they viewed as northern barbarians, such as the Gauls

and Germans. Not even Hannibal, who terrorized Rome at the end of the third century BC by leading his army unchecked through mainland Italy for three years, succeeded in taking Rome itself. He slaughtered thousands of Roman troops and inflicted on the Roman army some of the most stunning defeats they had ever sustained, but Rome itself remained untouched.

The Gauls in northern Italy were eventually overcome by the Roman capture of Milan and the defeat of the Gallic tribe of the Insubres, which allowed the Romans to create the province they named Cisalpine Gaul. During the second century BC a new Roman province of Transalpine Gaul was created in what is now southern France. The Romans simply named this region *Provincia*, meaning 'The Province', so giving us the origin of modern Provence. Southern Gaul by this time was becoming more Romanized and urbanized. Rome imported raw materials from Gaul and the Gauls, luxury goods from the Romans.

JULIUS CAESAR

Caesar was an astute politician who had realized that in the Rome of the first century BC military success was an important path to personal political power and influence. A war, therefore, was not simply something that could promote his own power, if and when one came along, but something he needed badly as a career opportunity. Like many successful politicians throughout history, Caesar knew how to create an opportunity when none presented itself in the ordinary course of events. To achieve the high office he enjoyed in the middle of the century he had spent extravagantly on entertaining the people and winning favour with the powerful, and consequently was heavily in debt. He had also annoyed many senators by his unorthodox methods of achieving power. He urgently needed to win a war that would bring him money, to pay his huge debts, and glory, through which he could establish himself as one of Rome's greatest men.

When he was created proconsul in 59 BC, Caesar's initial command was over Cisalpine Gaul and Illyria (what is now the Adriatic Balkan coast). For one such as he, however, from Cisalpine Gaul to Transalpine Gaul is but a step, and his command was extended to cover that region too. Once enmeshed in conquering the tribes of Gaul, he could extend his field of operations at will, as one opponent after another lined up to defy his territorial ambition. It has been estimated that during his nine years of operations in Gaul, Caesar sold into slavery over one million war captives. He came to the province in debt and left it one of the wealthiest men in the world.

Caesar was not simply a hugely successful politician. He had proved himself militarily in his youth while fighting Mithradates in the Near East, and, in middle age, his period in Spain in 61 BC showed that his early abilities had not been a fluke of youthful good fortune. The Gallic wars – and, let it be said, his own account of them – established his reputation for strategic and tactical brilliance, *celeritas* (speed of action and thought), organization of supplies, good use of Roman engineering skills, ambition and the personal magnetism that inspired soldiers of all ranks.

The battle of Bibracte was the first major confrontation in Caesar's Gallic campaigns. During the years 58–50 BC he would go on to conquer Gaul, make the first Roman expedition to Britain and put down widespread Gallic rebellions to bring the province fully and finally under Roman control. By the end, Gaul became several Roman provinces.

THE HELVETII
The first major confrontation of Caesar's Gallic wars was with the Helvetii, a Gallic tribe occupying what is now Switzerland. According to Caesar's account, they were led by one of their wealthiest members, Orgetorix, who convinced them that they were so superior in talents, abilities and physical resources that they were capable of ruling all of Gaul. He therefore persuaded the entire tribe, which Caesar numbered at 263,000, to destroy its towns and villages, put all their goods on carts and converge westward towards western Gaul.

THE GALLIC ARMY
Warfare was endemic among Gallic tribes and the Gallic army was based on the values of a warrior society. They did not have a guaranteed supply system, and so were unable to maintain armies for long periods, because the men were needed for labour in the fields. The army of the Helvetii probably included peasants as well as the warrior elite. Troops were not armed by their commanders but equipped themselves; hence their weapons were not uniform, and their effectiveness reduced. By contrast, each Roman legionary was armed as effectively as the richest of the Celtic warriors, and this difference in weaponry gave Rome a huge military advantage. The Gauls seemed to rely on breaking enemy lines at the start of a battle with infantry and cavalry charges. Their fighting style was to display themselves on the battlefield, either by fighting naked or by wearing elaborately decorated armour. The Gallic soldier was a little taller than the average Italian legionary.

THE ROMAN ARMY

By Caesar's time, the Roman army was essentially a professional force. Soldiers were trained, equipped and paid by the Roman state. Roman skirmishers – archers and slingers – supplemented the legions and provided flexibility in weapons and tactics. Caesar ensured that logistical support, in the form of supply lines of food and weapons, was well organized.

The main unit of the army was the legion. Most legionaries were volunteers drawn from the poorest citizens. The army provided these men with a living wage and the prospect of promotion. All legionaries were equipped in the same way. They were heavy infantrymen armed with a *pilum* (javelin), sword, body-shield, helmet and cuirass (breastplate).

In 88 BC most of Italy was granted Roman citizenship. Consequently the allied wings (*alae*) that had figured prominently in earlier Roman armies virtually disappeared, and Italians simply joined the legions as Roman citizens.

The cohort was the basic tactical unit, numbering approximately 480 men. Each cohort was divided into six centuries, and each century was commanded by a centurion. The most senior centurion commanded the entire cohort. The professional legion of this period consisted of ten cohorts, equal in size and uniformly equipped; so a legion at full strength had 4,800 men.

The cohort legion normally had a single commander who had to issue orders to, and direct, ten cohort commanders. Because all the cohorts were identical in size and equipment, they no longer needed to have a fixed position in the line; nor did the legion itself have to deploy in three lines, as in the past, but could adapt to the particular situation. Three lines were still common in the late Republic, with four cohorts in the first line and three each in the second and third, but we also hear of legions formed in two lines of cohorts, or four. A single line of cohorts was dangerously brittle and was used only in desperate

situations. The leader of the Roman auxiliary cavalry at Bibracte was a Gaul with connections to the Helvetii. Caesar was unsure of their loyalty.

PRELUDE TO BATTLE

The Helvetii, intent on their migration to western Gaul, were having considerable difficulty in pursuing their aims. Neighbouring tribes were understandably reluctant to let an entire people cross their lands unrestricted. Eventually they thought they had found an access point at Geneva and planned to mass on the banks of the River Rhône, then cross by existing fords.

In mid-March Caesar, then in Rome, received reports of the migration and rushed to Cisalpine Gaul. He had four legions under his control (VII, VIII, IX and X) and also auxiliary cavalry. He raised a further two legions in Cisalpine Gaul and took his assembled forces to Geneva, where he immediately destroyed a bridge that crossed the Rhône. The Helvetii asked him for permission to cross the river and move through the Roman *Provincia* into western Gaul. Their apparent readiness to ask favours from the Romans is surprising in the circumstances: they had been part of a Gallic force that had inflicted a humiliating defeat on a Roman army under Lucius Cassius in about 107 BC.

Caesar immediately used his forces to throw up a huge earthwork barrier almost 18 miles long and 16 feet high, which he fortified with watchtowers and garrisons, so that the Helvetii were effectively bottled up. The Helvetii sent further ambassadors to Caesar, who informed them that he could not allow them to pass into the Roman *Provincia* and that, if they tried to do so by force, he would attack them.

The Helvetii tried to cross the Rhône nonetheless, using boats and fords, but were unsuccessful. They then obtained the cooperation of the Sequani, a Gallic tribe based around their capital, Vesontio (modern Besançon), and succeeded in passing into western Gaul.

Caesar shadowed the migration of the Helvetii for weeks. There were several armed encounters; on one occasion, Caesar launched a surprise night attack at the River Saone, massacring many of the Helvetii. The Romans were highly skilled and professional, and were adept at manoeuvring at night.

Caesar was starting to run short of supplies, so he decided to march to the town of Bibracte, the central supply point for corn in the region. The Helvetii, perhaps seeing this as a sign of weakness, followed and harassed the Roman rear.

THE ARMIES DEPLOY

Caesar occupied a hill, sending his cavalry to delay the enemy. The four veteran legions deployed in the tradition triple *acies* halfway up the hill with the two newly recruited legions behind them. Caesar did not intend to use the latter troops, as he could not be sure

of their quality, but he reckoned that their numbers would impress the enemy. He dismissed his and his commanders' horses, as a grand gesture to his troops that he was personally committed to battle and neither could nor would run away. As the Romans readied themselves, the Helvetii drove back their cavalry. They deployed in dense lines at the bottom of the slope, with many of their families in carts and wagons behind them.

THE COURSE OF THE BATTLE

Caesar tells us that the Helvetii confidently advanced up the hill to meet the Roman line. The first attack by their main force was easily repulsed, because the Romans had the advantage of the slope and superior weaponry; their *pila*, which stuck into the enemy's shields, weighed them down and pinned them together or rendered their shields unusable. Many

TROOPS AT BIBRACTE

THE ROMANS – TOTAL 35,500

Romans legions, heavy infantry –30,000
(6 legions: 4 of these are veterans, legion
numbers: VII, VIII, IX and X; 2 are newly
recruited and inexperienced)

Numidian javelineers (skirmishers) – 500
Balearic slingers (skirmishers) – 500
Cretan archers (skirmishers) – 500
Auxiliary cavalry – 4,000

**THE HELVETII – TOTAL APPROXIMATELY
60,000**

Helvetii infantry – 41,000
Helvetii cavalry – 3,000
Allied heavy infantry (the Boii and Tulingi tribes) –
14,000
Allied cavalry (the Boii and Tulingi tribes) – 1,000

We do not have definitive sources for the Helvetii
army, so these numbers are an estimate only.

During his approximately 56 years Julius Caesar achieved sufficient fame to last him many lifetimes. If that were not enough, William Shakespeare's play telling the story of his betrayal and death in Rome in 44 BC has given his name such resonance that it is unlikely ever to be forgotten. Even without Shakespeare's contribution, though, Caesar would have lived in history because, quite simply, he was determined that he should. He was a highly effective self-publicist, revealing his flair in this field above all by the writing of his *Commentaries*, an endlessly self-flattering account of his conquest of Gaul between 58 and 50 BC. No opportunity is missed to display his courage, resourcefulness and cunning, and the unswerving admiration he wrests from even the most truculent of the Gauls.

Caesar's egotism had some justification, however. Even before his conquest of Gaul,

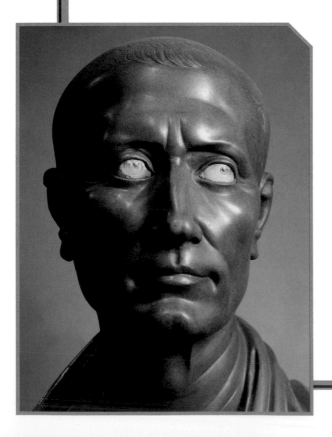

he had risen to the highest ranks of the Roman state, being elected consul in 59 BC. Earlier, he had been governor of what the Romans termed Farther Spain (now northern Spain) and had formed the first ruling triumvirate of the Roman state with the generals Pompey and Crassus in 60 BC.

As with many Roman military operations of the first century BC, Caesar's invasion of Gaul was a mixture of personal self-aggrandizement, novel wealth-creation schemes for himself and his family, furtherance of the glory of Rome and a genuine need to keep Rome's enemies at bay. The Gauls and Germans, long a threat to Rome, were in constant rivalry with one another and were pushing their neighbours into regions that infringed Roman territory.

Overall control of Gaul was, therefore, obviously in Rome's interest. Caesar initially achieved that control with great speed, systematically defeating the Helvetii, the Suebi under Ariovistus and the Nervii, all by 57 BC. He achieved effective domination of Gaul in not much more than a year. Longer-term domination, however, was to prove more elusive. In the years up to 52 BC there was a series of uprisings by the Gauls, to which the Romans responded with ever more punitive retaliatory strikes. Caesar's revenge for those attacks could be vicious; on one occasion he had the leader of an insurgent Gaulish tribe publicly flogged to death.

By 52 BC the situation in Gaul was so dangerous for the Romans that Caesar, returning from his winter quarters in northern Italy into what is now Provence, did not dare summon his legions there from their more northerly camps, because he was afraid that, without him there to lead them, they would be attacked *en route*. Instead, he himself quickly travelled north with a small force to join them. He then engaged in a year-long struggle with Vercingetorix, chief of the Averni. This second phase of the subjugation of Gaul saw several colossal confrontations between the Gauls and the Romans, notably at the sieges of Avaricum (now Bourges), Gergovia and Alesia.

The Gauls had learned a great deal from the Romans about military planning and engineering, and deployed against them the same carefully thought-through manoeuvres and siege weaponry that had proved so effective for the Romans. Notwithstanding, the fighting was utterly savage. It was Caesar's proud boast that out of the 40,000 Gauls at the siege of Avaricum only 800 escaped.

Despite his own great courage and resourcefulness, Vercingetorix could not defeat Caesar. His penalty was particularly hideous – and particularly Caesarean. He was brought as a prisoner to Rome, held there for six years, exhibited publicly as a defeated enemy in a Roman triumph and then executed.

When Caesar began his term of command in Gaul, only one legion was stationed there. By 50 BC there were ten, although they were smaller than was normal in the Roman army of the time: Caesar's Gallic legions tended to number about 3,500 men. He himself acknowledges that, at critical points in his campaign, such as the siege of Alesia, he would have been defeated by the weight of Gallic numbers had he not had at his disposal the tremendous skills of the Roman engineers, who planned and executed the elaborate earthworks dug during the siege.

Although it did not vanquish all opposition to Roman rule in Gaul, Caesar's defeat of Vercingetorix deprived the Gaulish insurgency movement of a rallying point. Thereafter, Roman armies were able to defeat their foes one by one, and Caesar could justifiably claim to have subdued Gaul.

Helvetii were killed or wounded, and their confidence evaporated. After a while they were forced back, though this may possibly have been a feint.

As the Roman cohorts pursued the retreating Helvetii, the latter's allies, from the tribes of the Boii and Tulingi, who formed the rearguard and had arrived at the battle late, swept around the baggage wagons and outflanked the Roman right. The Helvetii then renewed the fight, and now the Romans were surrounded. Infantry combat at close quarters ensued. The brilliant tactical flexibility of the legion enabled Caesar to order the rear line of cohorts to turn around, so that the legions were fighting on two fronts.

Fighting continued for about five hours. The Helvetii were pressed further and further back; the Boii and Tulingi were forced back against the wagons and slaughtered, along with all the women and children who had been left with the baggage carts. The Roman reserves on the hill were never engaged.

AFTERMATH

According to Caesar, 130,000 of the Helvetii survived the battle and marched for four days west to the territory of the Lingones (modern Langres). Roman casualties must have been considerable, because Caesar rested his army for three days before pursuing the Helvetii. In the meantime, he sent letters to the Lingones requesting them not to assist the Helvetii. When he caught up with them, the Helvetii promptly surrendered. Caesar ordered the survivors to return home to Switzerland. He claims that of the 263,000 Helvetii and 105,000 members of other tribes that accompanied them, totalling 368,000 people, only 110,000 returned, but we should be sceptical about those numbers.

Caesar had made a resounding start to his conquest of Gaul, but many battles, and tens of thousands of dead bodies, were to follow.

PHARSALUS 48 BC

BACKGROUND

A decade before the battle of Pharsalus, Julius Caesar, Pompey and Crassus had joined together in Rome to form a triumvirate, a ruling council of three men. It was a secret alliance designed to dominate the Roman Republic and divide political and military influence between the three men. Pompey had married Caesar's daughter Julia to cement the bond, but, over time, the relationship between Caesar and Pompey changed from one of friendship and political alliance to one of suspicion and bitter rivalry. In 54 BC Julia died in childbirth.

The Roman army was becoming a highly important factor in the political balance in Rome. In the years immediately preceding the wars in Gaul, the rules for admission to the army had changed: soldiers could be recruited from the very poor, and the Senate no longer provided land for soldiers upon discharge. Soldiers thus became more loyal to generous commanders, who allowed them to plunder conquered territories and so enrich themselves. Consequently the army was a power-base for charismatic leaders. Caesar's legions were fanatically loyal to him because he had given them glorious victories and rich rewards. Such popularity with the nation's military was a powerful political weapon.

Caesar's command in Gaul came to an end in about 50 BC. To avoid prosecution by his enemies on his return to Rome, Caesar demanded that he be made a designated consul while still in command of his armies in Gaul. Pompey refused to assent to this, and the Senate was deeply divided over the question. After much debate, the Senate declared war on Caesar in 49 BC. Four days later Caesar made his famous crossing of the River Rubicon with his armies behind him. The civil war had begun.

THE CIVIL WAR UNTIL PHARSALUS

Caesar advanced quickly through Italy. Pompey and most of the senior magistrates left Rome, declaring that it could not be defended.

The first clash between the two sides occurred at Corfinum, in central Italy, east of Rome (near modern Corfinio). Domitius Ahenobarbus, the candidate whom the Senate had selected to replace Caesar in Gaul, held the city against Caesar with 30 cohorts under his command. This action was against the wishes of Pompey, who wanted Ahenobarbus and his troops to march south to join him at Capua. Caesar mustered two legions and some Gallic cavalry and surrounded the town. Ahenobarbus panicked and his cohorts mutinied and surrendered. Caesar captured Ahenobarbus and pardoned him. The ordinary soldiers and most of the officers joined Caesar's army.

Pompey, now outnumbered in Italy, planned to cross to Greece, since he had many loyal client

Greece and they lacked leadership. Caesar is reported to have said that he went first to fight an army without a leader, before going to fight a leader without an army.

After an extended campaign at Ilerda (modern Lérida) in Spain, Caesar triumphed and the Pompeian leaders surrendered. Some of their army were recruited into Caesar's and the rest disbanded. Two legions in Farther (northern) Spain surrendered. In a few months, Caesar had conquered Spain with minimal loss of life. He appointed his own governor in the province and returned to Italy, on the way accepting the surrender of Massilia (near modern-day Marseilles).

By January 48 BC Caesar was ready to cross to Greece with seven legions and 500 cavalry and pursue Pompey there. This was a gamble, because he did not have a strong enough fleet to take on Pompey's ships if he was attacked at sea. Luckily, Pompey did not expect him to cross in January, when the weather was likely to be bad, and Caesar did not meet any opposition.

In Greece Caesar was isolated and outnumbered, although four more legions were on their way to him under the command of Mark Antony. By now Pompey had nine legions at his disposal, as well as 5,000 light infantry and 7,000 cavalry. Pompey's men were well provisioned, whereas Caesar's had to make do with what they could glean from local communities. It was not until 10 April that Mark Antony managed to bring the rest of his legions across the Adriatic. Caesar now had 11 legions, but was still outnumbered and still had supply problems.

He attacked one of Pompey's major supply centres at the port city of Dyrrachium (modern Durazzo), on the northern Greek coast. Outmarching the enemy, he infiltrated his army between Pompey and the city, although he was unable to seize the city itself. Both armies built siegeworks. After a long siege Caesar suffered a serious defeat. The war could have been ended there and then, but Pompey allowed him to escape. As recorded by Suetonius, a Roman historian

kingdoms in the east that could provide him with troops. His plan was to go east, recruit and train a large army and deal with Caesar later. Many Romans felt abandoned by his departure. He moved south to the port of Brundisium (modern Brindisi, the principal port for reaching Greece from Italy) and, while many of his army crossed to Greece, remained there with two legions. Caesar's engineers started constructing a huge mole, or harbour earthwork, to block access to the harbour. Pompey's fleet returned before the mole was complete and succeeded in evacuating Pompey and the remainder of his troops. In less than two months, Caesar had taken control of Italy, but he did not have a fleet and so could not immediately pursue Pompey to Greece.

Rather than fight Pompey directly, Caesar went overland to Spain from April to August 49 BC to attack and defeat legions loyal to Pompey there. These were the best of Pompey's troops, but Pompey was in of the first century AD, Caesar contemptuously remarked after the battle, 'Today the war would have been won by the enemy if they had a man who knew how to conquer.'

CAESAR IN 48 BC

At this point in his career Caesar was in his early 50s and at the peak of his abilities: a maverick operator, unpredictable, charismatic, a master of PR and a highly experienced and successful military commander. His strategy in the Roman civil wars was based on rapid offensive action, sometimes in the face of daunting odds. It was a very Roman tactic, one that the Roman people greatly admired in their commanders. Throughout the civil wars desertions from Pompey's army were common, but none are recorded from Caesar's forces. He was fighting this war with a clear and unambiguous objective: to protect his own personal honour, status and prestige.

POMPEY

Pompey, the leader of the forces loyal to the Roman Senate, was a very experienced military commander, and he showed great energy in training his newly recruited army, but by the time of Pharsalus he was probably past his prime. He had not been on campaign for 13 years, while Caesar was fresh from ten years' fighting in Gaul. In his youth Pompey had been a bold and brave commander, though he had a habit of turning up at the last minute and stealing others' glory.

He had many powerful Roman senators in his camp, which undermined his position as leader because they urged him to action which he might otherwise not have taken – or not, at least, at the time when it was suggested. His troops were from many different nations and had had no practice at fighting together as a unit. Their morale was also dangerously high, particularly after defeating Caesar at Dyrrachium, but they did vastly outnumber Caesar's army.

THE ROMAN ARMY

Both Pompey's and Caesar's troops were Roman-trained and Roman-led, so Pharsalus was a battle between two sides with the same military frame of reference. The main unit of the army continued to be the legion. All legionaries were equipped in the same way. The legionaries were heavy infantrymen armed with a *pilum* (javelin), sword, body-shield, helmet and cuirass (breastplate).

The cohort was the basic tactical unit and numbered approximately 480 men. A legion at full strength had 4,800 men. The cohort legion was flexible. It had a single commander who issued orders to ten cohort commanders. Because all the cohorts were identical in size and equipment, they could adapt to the particular situation. Three lines of battle were still common in the late Republic, with four cohorts in the first line and three each in the second and third. Well-trained and well-led legionaries in this period proved themselves capable of taking on and beating almost any opposition. They consistently defeated far larger opponents.

CAVALRY

Cavalry are vulnerable after a charge, even a successful one, because they tend to lose formation. To combat this, it is usual to keep some cavalry in reserve. Pompey, whose cavalry far outnumbered Caesar's at Pharsalus, made the mistake of deploying his cavalry too close together. When they met with success in a charge, therefore, they lost formation and degenerated into a mob. Pompey kept no cavalry in reserve.

PRELUDE TO THE BATTLE

After Dyrrachium, Caesar marched south into Thessaly, chiefly to search for food, which his armies desperately needed. His troops found fresh supplies and regained strength. Pompey believed that he should avoid open confrontation with Caesar, instead

attempting to wear him down by depriving him of supplies, but he was under tremendous pressure from the senators in his camp to meet Caesar in battle and finish things once and for all.

In early August, the two armies camped near each other on the plain of Pharsalus. They spent several days manoeuvring and offering formal challenges to battle. Pressure grew for Pompey to fight. On the morning of 9 August, Caesar was preparing to move camp to a place where he could more easily find food, when he noticed that Pompey's army had advanced further from their camp than usual. He quickly ordered his men to form in columns, wearing only battle equipment. They marched up, formed and faced the enemy.

HOW THE ARMIES DEPLOYED

Caesar set his army in the usual Roman formation of three lines, with his most experienced units on the flanks. Mark Antony was in command on the left, Cn. Domitius Calvinus in the centre and L. Cornelius Sulla on the right. Caesar spent most of the battle with Legio X, his favourite unit, on the right. The cavalry were massed on the right.

Pompey's army was larger. He also deployed his cohorts in three lines, but with an enormous force of 7,000 cavalry on the left supported by archers and slingers. In the centre were his legions from Syria, on the right his legions from Cilicia and some troops from Spain. Ahenobarbus was in command on the left,

TROOPS DEPLOYED AT PHARSALUS

CAESAR'S ARMY – TOTAL 24,000
Legions (all heavy infantry) – 22,000 (there were 80 under-strength cohorts, equalling 8 legions)
Cavalry – 1,000
Light infantry – 1,000

POMPEY'S ARMY – TOTAL 55,200
Legions, all heavy infantry – 45,000
(110 cohorts = 11 legions)
Archers – 3,000
Slingers – 1,200
Cavalry – 7,000

Scipio in the centre and Afranius on the right. The main line was very deep: each cohort was deployed in ten ranks.

Pompey had ordered his infantry not to advance, but to stay still and throw their *pila* when the enemy was within range. He knew his legionaries were not as effective as Caesar's. He planned to win the battle with his cavalry, by smashing Caesar's cavalry and wheeling around to attack the flank and rear of Caesar's infantry.

To counter the obvious superiority of Pompey's cavalry, Caesar took a single cohort from the third line of each of his legions and stationed it behind his cavalry, invisible to the enemy. For the battle Caesar's men were given the password 'Venus, Bringer of Victory', while Pompey's army had the password 'Hercules, Unconquered'.

THE COURSE OF THE BATTLE

Caesar's front line advanced while Pompey's infantry remained in position and his cavalry surged forwards. Caesar's cavalry gave way. During the charge Pompey's cavalry lost their cohesion and merged into one great mass, too closely packed to fight effectively. Caesar ordered his fourth line, the back-up legionaries, to attack, causing immediate panic among Pompey's cavalry, who stampeded to the rear. Pompey's supporting light infantry were abandoned and massacred or dispersed by Caesar's legionaries. Pompey's main attack had failed.

Meanwhile, the main infantry lines engaged. Caesar's men had charged as usual and then noticed that Pompey's infantry was not moving. To prevent them losing formation, the centurions halted the line, displaying their superb discipline. They reformed and charged again. When they were within 50 feet of the enemy they threw their missiles, then charged with drawn swords. A fierce struggle followed. The second line of infantry was drawn in. The fourth line of

Caesar's infantry, the one backing up the cavalry, attacked the exposed flank of Pompey's infantry, throwing it into disorder.

Caesar ordered his third line to advance. The pressure on Pompey's army was now too much. At first they retreated slowly but more and more of the units dissolved, until the retreat was total.

AFTERMATH

Caesar made sure that as many as possible of his enemy's legionaries were spared, but he allowed his troops to massacre the foreign auxiliaries. Pompey had left the battlefield almost as soon as his cavalry were swept away. As the defeat became obvious, he put aside his general's cloak and rode for the coast; at least, this is the account given in sources favourable to Caesar.

Of Pompey's army, 24,000 were imprisoned and 15,000 killed. Nine eagles, the legions' standards, were captured. Most of Pompey's army was pardoned, including M. Junius Brutus, who would later be one of the leading conspirators in Caesar's assassination.

Caesar claimed that he lost only 200 men and, because of their typically aggressive style of leadership, 30 centurions. Having sent Mark Antony back to Italy, he pursued Pompey to Egypt, where Pompey was tricked and murdered by a representative of the Egyptian king, who was unwilling to give help to an enemy of Caesar. When Caesar arrived in Alexandria, an envoy from the Egyptian king presented him with Pompey's head and signet ring. Caesar is reported to have wept. He gave honourable burial to Pompey's body. While he was in Egypt Caesar embarked on an affair with the 21-year-old queen Cleopatra.

Caesar's eventual success in the civil wars brought about the death of the Roman Republic, a system designed to prevent any single politician from becoming too powerful. Thereafter no Roman could oppose him, and political power in Rome was solely his. This led to his assassination and further civil war.

centurion

In a standard legion of Caesar's time there were 59 centurions: five in the first cohort of the legion and 54 in the remaining nine cohorts. The five centurions in the first cohort (*primi ordines*) were ranked, in descending order, as *primus pilus*, *princeps*, *hastatus*, *princeps posterior* and *hastatus posterior*. The six centurions in each of the other nine cohorts were ranked as *pilus prior*, *pilus posterior*, *princeps prior*, *princeps posterior*, *hastatus prior* and *hastatus posterior*.

By the time of the battle of Pharsalus, centurions were professional soldiers, like the ordinary legionary (*miles gregarius*). All centurions were of equal rank except the *primus pilus*, who took part in councils of war with the generals. The primary role of centurions was to maintain discipline among the ordinary soldiers and provide leadership in battle. Despite this apparently limited role, however, the generals depended heavily on the support of their centurions, and Caesar clearly went to great lengths to win their support. During his pursuit of the Gallic chieftain Ariovistus, for example, Caesar remarks that his troops became so despondent about their prospects of defeating

the enemy that every soldier made out a will, and the camp was full of rumours that, should Caesar call for the army to march, it would refuse to do so. Caesar's solution to the problem was to summon all the centurions and address them in a group. He made an eloquent speech and – in his own account, at least – the centurions were so convinced by his arguments that they became much more positive in their readiness to go into battle. Leaving aside the issue of how far Caesar wrote up his speech later, the mere fact that he felt it important to speak directly to the centurions shows how vital they were to a general's success in war.

Centurions were distinguished from ordinary soldiers by dress, both to denote their rank and to be visible in the chaos of battle. A centurion's helmet was decorated with a transverse (ear-to-ear) crest rather than a front-to-back one like the ordinary soldier's. He also carried a short stick, sometimes used to deal out corporal punishment. Centurions' armour was generally more richly decorated than the common soldiers', and they wore their swords on the right rather than left side.

WATLING STREET

AD 61

BACKGROUND

When the Romans invaded and occupied Britain, the Iceni tribe, from what is now East Anglia, quickly allied themselves with the invaders, seeking protection from their hostile neighbours. The Iceni paid tribute to Rome but continued to be ruled by their own kings. When the Iceni king Prasutagas died, however, he named the Roman emperor as co-heir to his kingdom along with his daughters. Roman agents moved to expropriate Iceni lands and to disarm the tribe. When Prasutagas' widow, Queen Boudicca, protested, the Romans had her flogged and her daughters raped.

The exact sequence of events is unknown, but soon afterwards the whole region (present-day Suffolk, Norfolk and Cambridgeshire) boiled over into rebellion. Boudicca mustered Iceni warriors as well as warriors from other tribes that had once been allied to Rome, such as the Tinovantes, who inhabited what is now Suffolk and Essex. It is recorded in both the main sources that all kinds of supernatural phenomena occurred when the revolt of the Iceni began. The Roman statue of victory erected at Camulodunum (Colchester) fell down for no apparent cause and lay on the ground with its face turned away. Women rushed among the people, screaming and announcing impending ruin. In Roman centres, howling in a foreign accent was heard in the theatres. Near the mouth of the Thames a ruined city was seen beneath the surface of the water; the sea ran red and, when the tide went out, human outlines were visible in the wet sand.

The warriors targeted Roman colonies at Colchester, London and St Albans and massacred virtually the entire detachment of the Ninth Legion (Hispana). The tribes had a bitter hatred of the Romans that showed itself in the massacre of any Roman civilians and collaborators they found in the cities and countryside. A focus of hatred among the Iceni was the Roman veterans who had been allowed to make a *colonia* (colony) at Colchester. These soldiers habitually mistreated the native Britons around them, abusing them by calling them cowards. The temple of the emperor cult also attracted exceptional anger, because it was seen as a symbol of oppression and abuse.

Such violent rage may have been at the heart of the very ugly tortures for which Boudicca's troops were apparently responsible. According to the Roman historian Cassius Dio (c. AD 150–235), Romans and those sympathetic to Rome, when captured by Boudicca's army were subjected to hideous abuse. Women of the most distinguished families were hung up naked, with their breasts cut off and sewed into their mouths to that they appeared to be eating them; afterwards they were impaled on sharp skewers driven lengthwise through their bodies. 'All this they did to the accompaniment of sacrifices, banquets, and wanton behaviour,' he concludes.

The morale and confidence of the Iceni were very high in the lead-up to the battle at Watling Street. They had been successful in their assaults on Roman power and had, so far, escaped unscathed.

While all this was going on in eastern and central England, Suetonius Paulinus, the Roman governor of Britain from AD 59 to 61, was blissfully unaware that events had taken such a bloody turn, since he was preoccupied with invading Anglesey, one of the last remaining centres of resistance to Roman rule in Britain. With the absence from central England of the legions that were being used in north Wales, resistance to the advances of the Iceni was much weaker than it might otherwise have been.

THE ROMAN ARMY

The professionalization of the army was completed under the rule of the Roman emperors. The cohort remained the basic tactical unit of the legion. In this period a legion consisted of:

✝ 9 cohorts, numbered II–X, each of 480 men in six centuries of 80 men apiece, each commanded by a centurion;

✝ the First Cohort of 800 men, divided into five double-sized centuries of 160 men;

✝ a small cavalry force of 120 men, used mainly as escorts or messengers.

Depending on the tactical situation the legion might also employ artillery. Light bolt-shooters such as *scorpios* (dart-throwers) and cheiroballistras were often used by Roman troops on the battlefield, sometimes mounted on mule-drawn carts for mobility.

In contrast to the Roman army of earlier times, the legions of the imperial period had permanent commanders, the Legionary Legates appointed by the emperor. These were senators, usually in their early thirties, who held the post for about three years. Next in rank below them were the senatorial tribunes, one for each legion. Having a permanent commander was a great advantage in maintaining consistency of discipline and a sense of the legion as a distinct entity with its own character and history.

An important feature of this period is the creation of the regularly paid, uniformed and equipped *auxilia* (auxiliary force), recruited from the ranks of foreign soldiers, for example from Germany or the Near East. These troops supported the Roman citizen legions by adding to their numbers and, in particular, by providing cavalry and other troops such as archers. Auxiliary infantry were organized into independent cohorts, but these cohorts were not combined into legion-sized formations.

Auxiliary cohorts usually numbered 480 men in six centuries, although a minority were increased to a strength of 800. The vast majority of auxiliary infantry were armoured heavy infantrymen equipped with javelins, swords, shields, mail armour and helmets. They were never armed with the heavier *pilum* and their uniform was kept distinct from that of the citizen legionaries, although their tactical function was similar.

Auxiliary cavalry were organized into similar-sized units, called not cohorts but *alae*. A cavalry *ala* normally consisted of about 512 men, occasionally 764. Auxiliary cohorts and *alae* were each commanded by a prefect.

TACTICS

In many respects the army of Nero's time employed a similar tactical system to the cohort legions of the first century BC. If anything, its flexibility had been enhanced by the creation of the well-trained and disciplined auxilia. In most respects auxiliary and legionary cohorts were tactically interchangeable, but the legionary cohorts, accustomed to working together and with a legate in command, were easier to control in battle than the independent auxiliary cohorts. The legions were especially suited to acting as a reserve (as, for example, at the battle of Mons Graupius in Scotland in AD 83) or, alternatively, could form the centre of the main attack, as in the defeat of Boudicca. Whenever possible the army deployed in at least two lines, and often three or more. Reserves were vitally important to maintaining the forward thrust of an attack. Once the forward troops became exhausted, they could fall back and regroup while reserves from the rear moved in to take their place.

Heavy infantry, whether legionaries or auxiliaries, continued to prove very effective. They were provided with excellent support by the professional auxiliary cavalry, and at times the latter played a more dominant role. Roman tactics for both infantry and cavalry continued to be very aggressive.

THE ROMAN GENERAL

According to the Roman historian Tacitus (c. AD 55–c. AD 117), Suetonius Paulinus was a very ambitious man who hoped to be considered one of the great generals of his day. His situation in the immediate aftermath of the Iceni revolt was bleak. If he lost the struggle against them, it was very likely that he would lose the entire province. If he survived and escaped, he would face the wrath of the emperor Nero, a man not noted for evenness of temper and balanced judgement at the best of times. Even the most phlegmatic of emperors would not take kindly to a governor who had lost him a province. To appear before Nero in such a guise was inviting not simply death but something a great deal worse for oneself and one's entire family. If Suetonius or his men were captured, then they faced only torture and death.

This was one of the most savage campaigns of the Roman period because of the sheer ferocity of the Britons' hatred for the Romans. The British atrocities prompted counter atrocities by the Romans, and a spiral of retribution ensued. After his victory over Boudicca, Paulinus was eventually recalled from Britain before the rebellion had been completely stamped out, because it was felt in Rome that the sheer violence of his reprisals against the Britons was destroying any chance of the two sides re-establishing a *modus vivendi*. Very few Roman governors were ever replaced on similar grounds.

THE BRITISH IN BATTLE

The British tried to make themselves look frightening in battle. They decorated themselves with the blue of woad tattoos, carried brightly painted shields and wore multicoloured clothes. Having washed their hair in lime they combed it up into spikes to exaggerate the size of their heads and appear bizarre and menacing. Noise was also employed in battle: it is recorded that the Gallic tribes, to whom many of the British tribes were related, habitually chose champions to walk out in front of the battle lines and shout challenges to the enemy. Many trumpets were carried and blown as loudly as possible.

Some Celtic warriors, mostly members of the retinue of chieftains, were quite well-equipped and skilful fighters, but they were in the minority. The bulk of the army consisted of peasants, many of whom may have had only improvised weapons, and most of whom had no real military experience. They were confident at the start of battle and individually ferocious but prone to panic if things went wrong. The Celts relied on a fierce infantry charge at the start of a battle to try to break the enemy line.

They also used chariots, which served two purposes: as a mobile missile platform and as transport for high-status warriors. The Celtic chariot carried a driver and a warrior armed with a javelin. As the chariot drove across the battlefield, the warrior hurled javelins, then jumped out to engage in battle on foot. In the meantime, the charioteer retired a short distance from the battle, waiting to collect the warrior and carry him to a place of retreat if required.

the Romans in Britain up to Boudicca

From Caesar's invasions of Britain in 55 and 54 BC until the abandonment of the country to its own defence by the emperor Honorius in AD 410, Roman culture and, above all, Roman legions were an integral part of the British way of life. But Roman rule was not universally popular, either immediately after Caesar's invasion or even a full century later when Boudicca revolted.

In the intervening period, Rome had determinedly expanded its hold on Britain. Caesar's two mini-invasions had given him some knowledge of Britain; his defeat of King Cassivellaunus allowed him to take hostages, who were then used as surety for taxes that Caesar levied on the British. Client relationships were also established with British tribes who were eager to enlist Roman assistance in struggles with their neighbours. For example, the Atrebates, south of the River Thames, welcomed the help of the Romans in limiting encroachments by the Catuvellauni from north of the river. These client relationships were strengthened by the emperor Augustus, but Britain came more completely under Roman rule after Claudius' invasion in AD 43. His legions, latterly led by Claudius himself, quickly subdued opposition in the southeast, and by AD 47 a line of Roman control ran from Exeter to the River Humber. A Roman *colonia* of legionary veterans was established at Camulodunum, the cult of the emperor was established and towns were founded.

The most important British tribes during this period were the Catuvellauni and Atrebates on each side of the Thames, the Iceni in what is now East Anglia, the Corieltavi in the Midlands, the Dobunni around Gloucestershire and the Durotriges in Dorset. Other, independent, tribes included the Dumnonii of Devon, the Brigantes in the north and the Silurii and Ordovicii in Wales.

Cassius Dio has left us with a very striking portrait of Boudicca and of her ability to express with great eloquence her hatred for the state of being enslaved by the Romans. Notice how skilfully Boudicca makes her points: she tells her people that, although they may have been ignorant about what the Romans had to offer, now they have seen it and they know it for what it is worth. She lists the Romans' abuses: theft, taxation on what is left, then further taxes every year. They would be better off as ordinary slaves, for they are sold only once. She clinches the argument by saying the Romans are cowards anyway: they cover themselves with armour because they're so terrified of being hurt.

'This woman [recounts Cassius Dio] assembled her army, to the number of some 120,000, and then ascended a tribunal which had been constructed of earth in the Roman fashion. In stature she was very tall, in appearance most terrifying, in the glance of her eye most fierce, and her voice was harsh; a great mass of the tawniest hair fell to her hips; around her neck was a large golden necklace; and she wore a tunic of divers colours over which a thick mantle was fastened with a brooch. This was her invariable attire. She now grasped a spear to aid her in terrifying all beholders and spoke as follows:

'"You have learned by actual experience how different freedom is from slavery. Hence, although some among you may previously, through ignorance of which was better, have been deceived by the alluring promises of the Romans, yet now that you have tried both, you have learned how great a mistake you made in preferring an imported despotism to your ancestral mode of life, and you have come to realize how much better is poverty with no master than wealth with slavery. For what treatment is there of the most shameful or grievous sort that we have not suffered ever since these men made their appearance in Britain? Have we not been robbed entirely of most of our possessions, and those the greatest, while for those that remain we pay taxes? Besides pasturing and tilling for them all our other possessions, do we not pay a yearly tribute for our very bodies? How much better it would be to have been sold to masters once for all than, possessing empty titles of freedom, to have to ransom ourselves every year! How much better to have been slain and to have perished than to go about with a tax on our heads! Yet why do I mention death? For even dying is not free of cost with them; nay, you know what fees we deposit even for our dead. Among the rest of mankind death frees even those who are in slavery to others; only in the case of the Romans do the very dead remain alive for their profit. Why is it that, though none of us has any money (how, indeed, could we, or where would we get it?), we are stripped and despoiled like a murderer's victims? And why should the Romans be expected to display moderation as time goes on, when they have behaved toward us in this fashion at the very outset, when all men show consideration even for the beasts they have newly captured?

'"Have no fear whatever of the Romans; for they are superior to us neither in numbers nor in bravery. And here is the proof: they have protected themselves with helmets and breastplates and greaves and yet further provided themselves with palisades and walls and trenches to make sure of suffering no harm by an incursion of their enemies."'

THE ROMAN ARMY – TOTAL 10,000
Roman legionary cohorts (infantry) – 5,000
Allied heavy infantry – 2,500
Allied light infantry archers – 500
Allied heavy cavalry – 1,000
Allied medium cavalry – 1,000

THE ICENI – TOTAL 62,800
Chariots – 400 (with two men apiece)
Cavalry – 2,000
There was an estimated total of 60,000 infantry

PRELUDE TO THE BATTLE

According to Tacitus, when Paulinus heard about the revolt of the Iceni he marched his legions through the middle of Britain to London. Although the city was not a Roman *colonia*, and therefore not sanctified by the presence of a dedicated emperor-cult temple, it was still an important strategic point for Paulinus' grip on the country. Nonetheless, he decided that he had to sacrifice it for a greater tactical advantage. The Londoners begged Paulinus to defend the city, but he refused, as he did, too, for Verulamium (St Albans), knowing it was a soft target for the Iceni because it was not heavily defended. Paulinus then marched to the Midlands. His troops included Legion XIV, parts of Legions II and IX and about 4,500 auxiliaries, a total of just 10,000 men.

SITE OF THE BATTLE

Tacitus is very precise about the terrain on which the battle with the Iceni was fought, recording that Paulinus chose a spot surrounded by woods, with a narrow entrance that was protected in the rear by a thick forest. Thus positioned, Paulinus had no fear of being suddenly attacked from the sides or the back. The Iceni, he knew, could approach only from the front.

Despite the detail of his description of the battleground, Tacitus does not tell us whereabouts in Britain it was. Some authorities suggest Mancetter, a village near Atherstone in Warwickshire, as the most likely site. Mancetter, whose name means 'the place of chariots', was the location of a Roman fort on Watling Street, the major Roman road that stretched from London to Anglesey.

Boudicca and her warriors arrived on the battlefield in huge numbers. There was no organized line of battle, and individual warriors and groups of warriors milled around, displaying how many of them had come to fight. The Iceni and their allies were so sure of victory, reports Tacitus, that they placed their wives and families in wagons on the edges of the battlefield, wanting them to witness their great feats of arms.

THE COURSE OF THE BATTLE

According to Cassius Dio, Paulinus divided his army into three groups, because, even if he had created a single line only one man deep, it would not have stretched far enough to equal the front of the British army. Each of the three groups was formed into a densely packed, disciplined body. The Romans had the advantage of the high ground. As the Celts charged uphill at the Roman legionaries, Boudicca leading in her chariot, they were met with two volleys of javelins followed by a legionary counter-charge in two wedges, one of legionaries and the other of auxiliaries. Simultaneously, the Roman cavalry charged. The tribesmen were pushed backwards, into and beyond a narrow defile. The lie of the ground and the packed mass of non-combatants and wagons behind their position combined to trap the Celts and allow the legions and auxiliary cavalry to cut them to pieces.

AFTERMATH

It is estimated that no fewer than 80,000 Britons were indiscriminately slaughtered, because the women and children were targets of the Roman attack no less than the men who had gone to fight. 'Neither sex nor age was spared,' as Tacitus puts it. The Romans lost 400 and roughly the same number were wounded.

Boudicca died soon after the battle. The sources disagree about whether her death was the result of natural causes or of poison.

The defeat of such a large army inevitably signalled the end of the short-lived rebellion of the Iceni. Over the next 30 years, the Romans continued to expand their presence in Britain, fully conquering Wales and pressing far into Scotland.

MONS GRAUPIUS
AD 83

BACKGROUND

Mons Graupius was one of the largest battles of the Romans' 150-year struggle for domination of Britain. The first time the Roman army brought its might to Britain was when Julius Caesar led it there in 55 and 54 BC. He did not conquer the island or, indeed, do much more than fight a long-drawn-out struggle with Cassivellaunus, leader of the British tribes in the southeast. On his second expedition he brought five legions and 2,000 cavalry but then had to leave suddenly because of renewed tensions in mainland Europe. Full-scale invasion had to wait until the emperor Claudius arrived in AD 43. Britain then came much more under Roman rule.

After the suppression of Boudicca's rebellion in AD 61, the Romans engaged in savage reprisals, trying to virtually wipe out any tribe or group that had sided with her. Reinforcements arrived from Germany to replace the legionaries killed in the rebellion. But over the next 20 years the Roman authorities tried much harder to build bridges with the British tribes. More work was done at Roman expense, and new towns such as Bath were founded.

In AD 77 or 78 Cn. Julius Agricola became governor of Britain. Agricola had been a junior officer in the army of Paulinus, the victor at Watling Street, and some of Paulinus' habits seem to have rubbed off on him. Almost from the moment he arrived in Britain, he set about attacking the Ordovicii, a tribe living in north Wales, who had recently slaughtered a troop of Roman cavalry. Others thought it better to wait, not least because winter was setting in, but Agricola went ahead and wiped out the Ordovicii. Then, perhaps because he was already in North Wales, Agricola decided to take up another of Paulinus' preoccupations and attempt to complete the conquest of Anglesey. Paulinus had been in the middle of that process when Boudicca's revolt took place, and had to abandon the island. Agricola was plainly a resourceful commander: having no boats with which to ford the strait between Anglesey and the mainland, he singled out from among his men those who knew from past experience how to swim with their horses. They duly swam over with horses and equipment and took the inhabitants of Anglesey completely by surprise. They surrendered and Agricola found himself master of the island. With those two feathers in his cap, he could feel he had begun his governorship well.

Although he had learned much from Paulinus, Agricola showed by his behaviour in Britain that he also understood what Paulinus had done wrong. He set about getting rid of corruption among Roman officials and Britons who were in Roman pay. There were many abuses, particularly in the collection of taxes. People were forced to buy corn, on which tax was levied, at hugely inflated prices, or from granaries that were many miles from their homes, even though nearer

AGRICOLA'S ARMY

When Claudius invaded Britain in AD 43, he brought four full legions with him: II Augusta, XIV Gemina Martia, XX Valeria Victrix and IX Hispana. They had all previously been stationed on the Rhine, except IX Hispana, which came from the Danube. With these regular legionaries also came auxiliaries, probably in equal numbers. If the legions were approximately 5,000–6,000 strong then, assuming the same number of auxiliaries, the total force would have been at least 40,000 men. Legio XIV was recalled in AD 68 and withdrawn from Britain completely in AD 70, but most of these regiments would stay in Britain until about AD 400, a period of almost 350 years.

These troops, then, were the backbone of the forces Agricola had at his disposal when he arrived in Britain.

The professional Roman soldiers of this period were constantly trained to use their weapons, using the methods originally devised to train gladiators. The cohort remained the basic tactical unit of the legion. In this period a legion consisted of:

✝ 9 cohorts, numbered II–X, each of 480 men, in six centuries of 80 men apiece, each commanded by a centurion;

✝ the First Cohort of 800 men, divided into five double-sized centuries of 160 men;

✝ a small cavalry force of 120 men, used mainly as escorts or messengers.

Depending on the tactical situation the legion might also employ artillery. Light bolt-shooters such as scorpios (dart-throwers) and cheiroballistras were often used by Roman troops on the battlefield, sometimes mounted on mule-drawn carts for mobility.

The legions of the imperial period had permanent commanders, the Legionary Legates appointed by the emperor. These were senators, usually in their early thirties, who held the post for about three years. Directly below them in rank were the senatorial tribunes, one for each legion.

granaries were full. Agricola also followed a strategy of attacking defended centres of resistance against Roman rule, while at the same time initiating building projects for new towns and temples, entirely paid for by Rome, to show the British that the Romans were not there simply to tax them mercilessly without giving anything back. He also picked out children from rich families and had them educated in Roman manners, language and learning. As a result, Tacitus tells us, acquiring Latin became all the rage among the wealthy families of Britain.

Agricola then began to push Roman control north, and in AD 79 brought his legions into Scotland, progressing as far north as the River Tay.

An important feature of this period is the creation of the regularly paid, uniformed and equipped *auxilia* (auxiliary force), recruited from the ranks of foreign soldiers, for example from Germany or the Near East. These troops supported the Roman citizen legions by adding to their numbers and, in particular, by providing cavalry and other troops such as archers. Auxiliary infantry were organized into independent cohorts, but these cohorts were not combined into legion-sized formations.

Auxiliary cohorts usually numbered 480 men in six centuries, although a minority were increased to a strength of 800. The vast majority of auxiliary infantry were armoured heavy infantrymen equipped with javelins, swords, shields, mail armour and helmets.

Auxiliary cavalry were organized into similar-sized units, called *alae*. A cavalry *ala* consisted of about 512 men. Auxiliary cohorts and *alae* were each commanded by a prefect.

Because he held his legions in reserve, only a small part of Agricola's army at Mons Graupius consisted of legionaries, the bulk being non-citizen auxiliaries. Auxiliary infantry were armoured and fought in close order like the legionaries, but, lacking the higher command structure of the legions, were less easy to control in large numbers during a battle. The auxiliaries at Mons Graupius were mainly from the Germanic tribes of Batavia (modern Holland) and Tungria (Tongres in modern Belgium). According to Tacitus, Agricola also pitched Briton against Briton by bringing into battle with him British troops who had proved their loyalty to Rome. Like the Celts, the Romans used noise, or an absence of noise until the critical moment, to intimidate the enemy.

Tacitus also records that Agricola wanted to win the battle using only the auxiliaries because the victory would be all the greater if no drop of Roman blood were spilled. Of course, Tacitus may have invented this to make Agricola look good; he had, after all, married Agricola's daughter.

THE BRITISH GENERAL

We are told that the leader of the British was called Calgacus, or Calgaich. Tacitus, in his account of the battle, gives him a wonderful speech that makes us feel very sympathetic towards the British. Calgacus stood up before his troops and said:

'We, the last men on earth, the last of the free, have been shielded till today by the very remoteness and the seclusion for which we are famed. We have enjoyed the impressiveness of the unknown. But today the boundary of Britain is exposed; beyond us lies no nation, nothing but waves and rocks and the Romans, more deadly still than they, for you find in them an arrogance which no reasonable submission can elude. Brigands of the world, they have exhausted the land by their indiscriminate plunder, and now they ransack the sea. The wealth of an enemy excites their cupidity, his poverty their lust of power.'

The British had the advantage of being on home ground. Their troops were largely from the Caledonii, but were probably also drawn from other tribes in what is now northern Scotland. Tacitus records that the Caledonii looked like the fair-haired warriors of Germany, with 'reddish hair and large limbs'. By the time of Agricola's campaigns the Celtic tribes in this region had a social system sophisticated enough to offer wide-scale resistance to the Romans, but they respected the might of the Roman legions and were careful not to engage in battle rashly.

THE BRITISH IN BATTLE

How the British tribes behaved in battle depended largely on the situation. They were loosely organized in warrior bands of families and neighbours, with the most highly motivated and best-equipped warriors in front and the poorer and less enthusiastic in the rear.

They were especially formidable at the start of a battle, especially in the first charge, when their terrifying appearance and the fighting prowess of the bolder men in the front ranks could sweep an enemy away. But if that tactic failed to work they often lacked the stamina to carry on, and it was easy for the less motivated men in the rear to vanish and avoid the fight.

Most importantly, their lack of formal training or group discipline meant that the warrior bands were very difficult to manoeuvre as a fighting force, finding it hard to change front or direction during a battle. That problem was exacerbated at Mons Graupius by the size of the army, which was almost certainly larger than any the tribes had ever assembled before. A plan of action would have to be simple if the disparate parts of the army were not to become confused and begin acting independently.

Almost all the British were unarmoured, though a few of the chieftains may have had mail armour and a helmet. Tacitus remarks that the British carried particularly small shields.

CELTIC CHARIOTS

Chariots were not intended to charge headlong into formed enemy units. They were basically missile platforms and a means of transporting aristocratic warriors swiftly to and from the fighting line. By this date they were an outdated tool of warfare, but they could still have an effect and the Romans could not ignore them.

THE SITE OF THE BATTLE

No one is absolutely sure where the battle of Mons Graupius took place: a number of sites have been suggested. It is most likely that the battle was fought between present-day Aberdeen and Stonehaven, near what are now called the Grampian Mountains. The remains of Roman forts and camps have been found in the region.

PRELUDE TO BATTLE

The British had been gathering in the region for at least some days before the battle, sending messengers in all directions, appealing for warriors to come forward to meet the Romans. According to Tacitus, 30,000 troops were gathered and still more kept arriving, the bravest and most skilled warriors that could be found. Calgacus made his great speech, and gradually the British formed themselves into a line of battle. They had absorbed lessons from fighting the Romans and arranged their troops on the high ground, to give them the advantage. The infantry lined up the slopes, while the chariots, cavalry and skirmishers deployed on the flat ground in front. At the top of the slope, looking down on the whole battlefield, were the reserves.

Agricola deployed his auxiliaries for battle, placing the infantry in the centre and the cavalry on the flanks, with four squadrons of horse in reserve. To avoid being outflanked he spread his front line thin. He kept his legions in reserve, probably in front of the Roman camp.

THE COURSE OF THE BATTLE

The battle began with an exchange of missiles, the Romans throwing their javelins at the British, who succeeded in warding them off with their swords and shields. Then Agricola pushed forward his Batavians and Tungrians, calling on them to assault the British with their swords, stabbing them in the eyes. The auxiliaries hacked their way through, butchering as they went, even leaving unwounded Britons behind them because they were moving so quickly. The British found it difficult to fend them off because, says Tacitus, their swords were not adapted to the close-quarter stabbing and gouging at which the auxiliaries were so skilled; furthermore, their shields were too small.

In the meantime, the Roman cavalry had destroyed the British chariot force and turned its attention to the British infantry. So many British were on the battlefield, however, that the Romans' progress began to slow; they simply could not chop their way through such an enormous number of men. It began to look as if the Romans might lose.

Now the British troops who had been waiting at the top of the hill began to make their way down and attack the Roman rear. Agricola, however, had been anticipating just such a move and sprang his surprise attack. He threw the four reserve squadrons of cavalry against the British as they came down the hill, and the tide of battle turned. The British ranks could no longer hold together but broke into smaller and smaller groups, surrounded and fighting desperately for their lives. Large groups fled before small numbers of Romans, Tacitus records, while others, having no weapons, simply threw themselves upon the Romans' swords.

Many of the British fled towards nearby woods, where they had the presence of mind to remain in hiding and ambush the Romans who were pursuing them. Agricola, however, rode down and organized his troops, telling them to encircle the woods, then sent in dismounted cavalry to finish off those who were still hiding. It was all over.

AFTERMATH

Body parts lay everywhere, says Tacitus, and the earth was soaked in blood. He puts the British dead at 10,000 and the Roman losses at 360. The countryside was deathly still, and there was not a sound anywhere.

It was nearly winter, and Agricola could not continue to campaign. The following year he was recalled to Rome by the emperor Domitian, who was extremely jealous of his achievements. Agricola died soon afterwards in mysterious circumstances. Despite his successes in Scotland, the lands beyond the Forth–Clyde isthmus remained largely free from Roman control.

Calgacus seemed to have survived the battle, but with the loss of so much life, and of crops as well, it must have been a grim winter for the tribes of Caledonia.

Supporting the legionaries' swords, spears and shields with missile weapons became increasingly the military practice among the Romans as the first century AD wore on. These weapons were often powered by ratchets and gears that allowed the users to draw back a driving support, like the cable in a crossbow, and release the projectile with enough force to smash through the thickest shield or the best-quality armoured breastplate. Each legion had a detachment responsible for maintaining and deploying such weapons.

Vegetius, a Roman writer of the fourth century AD, who left us one of the most complete records of Roman military practice in his book *De Re Militari*, tells us that legions owed their successes to such weapons as much as to the bravery of the legionaries. Every century had a *ballista* ('stone thrower'), constructed of wood, metal and rope and operated by pulling back a thick rope under tension on a wooden frame. When the rope was released it fired darts, arrows and stones at the enemy. A *ballista* was mounted on a cart drawn by mules and it was the duty of a special group of ten men to operate and maintain it. The larger the *ballista*, the more powerful it was and the more damage it could do. *Ballistae* were not only used to defend a camp when it was surrounded by earthworks and trenches but also placed in the rear of the battle line, from which vantage point they threw arrows and stones that could smash chariots, kill teams of chariot horses or cripple an individual warrior by destroying his shield and armour. Normally a legion had 55 *ballistae* at its disposal, and their combined firepower must have been utterly terrifying, sheaves of arrows hurtling towards the enemy at far greater speed than was possible with an ordinary bow.

As well as the *ballistae*, each legion had another fearsome weapon called the onager, or wild ass. This was a catapult that operated in principle very much like a huge mousetrap. A long, heavy wooden arm with a cup at the end was jointed to a flat wooden platform. The cup having been filled with stones, the arm was drawn back under tremendous tension as far as it would go; when it was released, the stones flew through the air at tremendous speed, falling some distance away on the enemy with crushing force. Onagers were made in different sizes: huge ones for use in sieges, when they would hurl enormous stones over the walls of cities and towns, smashing through buildings and walls, and smaller ones for use on the battlefield. Because they were generally larger than the *ballistae*, the onagers were mounted on carts drawn by oxen, which were much stronger than donkeys. There were usually ten onagers for each legion.

All in all, the legions had at their disposal a devastating range of firepower, which, being mobile, could be deployed in a flexible way. Small wonder, then, that legions with relatively few men could successfully defeat much greater numbers of enemies.

TROOPS AT MONS GRAUPIUS

**THE ROMAN ARMY – TOTAL 19,000
(THE LEGIONS, 6,000 OF THESE MEN,
WERE HELD IN RESERVE)**
3 Roman legions, heavy infantry – 6,000
Allied infantry – 8,000
Allied cavalry – 5,000

THE CALEDONII ARMY – TOTAL 30,000
Chariots – 250 chariots with 2 men each
Cavalry – 3,500
Infantry – 23,000
Infantry skirmishers – 3,000

ADRIANOPLE

AD 378

BACKGROUND

Adrianople was also known in the past as Hadrianopolis. Now called Edirne, it is a city in the westernmost part of Turkey, close to the borders with Greece and Bulgaria.

THE ROMAN EMPIRE IN THE FOURTH CENTURY AD

By the fourth century AD the Roman Empire stretched all the way from the western shores of Britain to the River Euphrates, in what is now Iraq. It was so enormous that it was impossible for one person or one government to control it: the city of Rome and an emperor based there were not enough. So in the early fourth century AD the empire was split into western and eastern halves, with an emperor for each. At the time of the battle of Adrianople, Flavius Valens was emperor in the East and his nephew Flavius Gratianus (Gratian) in the West.

The two empires, however, were not strong. Frequent civil wars during the third and fourth centuries AD had left the Roman frontier defences weak. The Rhine frontier was threatened by a confederation of Germanic tribes known as the Alamanni, and the Danube by the Quadi and their allies and by the Goths. The crisis occurred on the Danube, however, with the events that led up to the battle of Adrianople.

ROMAN–GOTH TENSIONS

The Romans became aware of the Goths as the latter expanded their territories in the third century AD and came into conflict with the Romans. In that period the Goths moved into Thrace and the area of Moesia in the Balkans. In AD 251 a Gothic army defeated a Roman army in the Dobruja region of the Balkans, killing the emperor, Decius. The Roman emperor Marcus Aurelius Claudius then defeated the Goths at Naissus, in the Balkans, in AD 269, leading to an uneasy peace that lasted for 100 years.

Troubles in Goth–Roman relations began developing again in the reign of the emperor Julian (AD 360–363) and continued to worsen after the Goths supported the army of Procopius, a rival to the imperial throne of Valens, Julian's successor. Valens then decided on pre-emptive military action to secure the Danube frontier and, in the late 360s, attacked Goth territory north of the Danube in a series of campaigns. His successes there did not entirely solve the problems, and a partial peace treaty was agreed in AD 369.

In the early 370s the Goths again migrated westwards towards the Danube; no one is quite sure why, but some suggest it was because groups of Huns to their east were expanding westwards, thus putting pressure on their territories. When the Goths and some bands of Alans and Huns on the move with them

arrived at the River Danube in AD 376, they knew
they could not cross it without Roman consent. The
Tervingi Goths therefore sought permission to cross
the Danube. Valens, then campaigning in Persia, was
enticed by the promise of Goth warriors becoming new
recruits to his armies, and so allowed the migration.
The Roman command on the Danube had no idea how
many refugees to expect, and did not know that over
the next few weeks tens of thousands of Goths would
enter Roman territory. The figures in the sources for
the migration are absurdly high, varying from 200,000
down to 90,000; modern estimates agree with the
lower figure.

Before the Tervingi Goths were allowed to cross the
river, the Romans disarmed them, but some weapons
slipped through, and later the Goths looted weapons
from the Romans. Most Goth horses were also
confiscated. Greuthungi, Alanic and Hunnic refugees,
who joined the crossing late when the Romans were
overstretched, were able to cross with their arms
and horses.

The Goths entering Roman lands were not
concerned with destroying Roman power, but rather
with creating a place for themselves within the
Roman system. However, the Romans did not have
the resources to feed and process the large numbers
of refugees, and the situation spiralled into anarchy.
The Goths are said to have resorted to eating dogs
and selling children into slavery. Starvation ensued.
According to some sources, this poor treatment was
a result of corruption and mismanagement by the
Roman frontier commanders, but others argue that
resources were simply overstretched.

When the Goth leaders near the Danube threatened
revolt, the Roman commander Lupicinus attempted to
murder them at a banquet. The leader, Fritigern, and
some others escaped. Not unreasonably outraged by
this attempt to wipe out their leaders, the Goths rose
in revolt against the Romans.

FRITIGERN

Fritigern seems to have been the sole leader of the
Goth clan of the Tervingi by the time of the battle
of Adrianople. He must have had great personal
leadership qualities and force of will to hold toget
her the coalition of disparate clans and tribes that
had poured into Roman territory. He was shrewd and
resourceful, an opportunist, striking when the time
was right and withdrawing when it was not. Skilled
as a strategist, he risked battle only when he knew
he could win. He had to persuade his followers of the
wisdom of any action; he could not simply issue orders
and expect them to be followed. His overall strategy
appears to have been to keep his people moving in
small groups, thereby easing the problems of food
supply and making it difficult for the Romans to detect
them. His ability to split his forces into small groups
and re-form them when necessary is impressive. He
moved cautiously, carried out proper reconnaissance
and kept his army supplied with food and equipment.
This was no mean logistical feat given the situation.

The other Gothic leaders were Alatheus and
Saphrax, who led the clan of the Greuthingi, but not
much is known about them. Saphrax may have been
a Hun. The Huns were a nomadic Turkic people from
Central Asia described by Ammianus, a historian
of the fourth century AD, as having 'squat bodies,
strong limbs and thick necks'.

VALENS

Valens had been made emperor of the Eastern Roman
Empire in AD 364 by his brother Flavius Valentinianus,
who was emperor of the West. History's verdict is that
Valens was not a skilled leader. He was almost fifty
when he fought at Adrianople, and he had spent much
of his tenure as emperor defending his territory in the
field. His decisions at Adrianople seem to have been
based on pride rather than tactical soundness. He
went into battle quickly because he did not want to

share the glory with his nephew Gratian, emperor of the Western Roman Empire, who was on his way with reinforcements.

Ammianus describes Valens as a faithful friend who maintained discipline in the army and was even-handed in his administration of the provinces under his control, but could be cruel and rather slow to take action.

THE GOTHIC ARMY

The Goths gathered near Adrianople were not so much an organized army as a whole society on the move, fighting with whatever weapons they could capture. The core of the army was the Gothic clan of the Tervingi; it also included the Greuthungi from further east, nomadic Huns and Alans, Gothic units from the Roman army, escaped Roman slaves, prisoners of war, deserters and gold miners. The Alans were a nomadic Aryan/Iranian people, described by Ammianus as 'tall, handsome, with yellowish hair and frighteningly fierce eyes'.

In order to diminish any threat they might pose, the Goths had been largely disarmed by the Romans as they crossed the Danube, so many of the weapons they used at Adrianople must have been stolen or captured afterwards from the Romans.

The Goths did not have clear divisions of cavalry and infantry. A warrior fought on horse or on foot as the situation demanded. They did not have as many cavalry in their army as historians used to assume. They were largely an infantry force and seem to have preferred fighting on foot, except where there was an advantage to fighting on horseback, as in the surprise attack of the Greuthungi at Adrianople.

Unlike many western Germanic people, the Goths seem to have made good use of missiles. The archers in particular proved a problem for the Romans. It appears that they formed part of the main body of troops, rather than being a distinct group of light infantry skirmishers. An account of the battle of Ad Salices in AD 377, when Fritigern defeated a small force of Valens' troops in the Balkans, testifies to the Goths' use of missiles and to their courage in battle with the Romans.

The Huns and Alans formed a distinct group at Adrianople and fought in their traditional manner as light mounted archers. They operated together and in similar ways, but ethnically were quite distinct. According to Ammianus the Huns were lightly equipped, very sudden in their movements, shot arrows tipped with sharp splinters of bone from a distance, and fought at close quarters without regard for their lives. While their opponents were fending off their sword-thrusts the Huns lassoed their limbs. The Alans, too, Ammianus says, were nomadic, and were active and nimble in their fighting style, in every way the equal of the Huns.

THE ROMAN ARMY OF THE LATE EMPIRE (C. AD 250–450)

At the time of Adrianople, the Roman army was both the Empire's biggest employer and the greatest drain on the imperial budget. Its organization had a huge impact on the economy of both the eastern and western empires.

The Roman legion had shrunk to approximately 1,000–1,200 men. There appear to have been no subdivisions equivalent to earlier groups such as maniples or cohorts. The entire legion fought as a single block. Auxiliary units were either about the same size as the legions or possibly half as large. Both legions and auxiliary units were usually brigaded with another unit of the same type, and these pairs tended to fight in support of each other.

There was a range of different cavalry units including *vexillationes* (about 600 men) and *scholae* (about 500). Other units may have been smaller, at around the 300–400 mark. There was a broad range of titles for the commanders of units.

The system of command and control followed in the armies of the later Empire was not best suited to the open battles of the past. The nodes of command were more widely dispersed and that made integrated communication throughout Europe's armies more difficult. The distinction between citizen and non-citizen Roman troops, important during the years of the Republic, was now so blurred that it no longer mattered; their equipment and training were virtually identical.

The defeat at Adrianople was largely caused by Valens' mistakes rather than the army's inefficiency. It may have reflected how unprepared a fourth-century Roman army was for operating in large numbers. It was a setback, but not an indication of a great decline in the quality of the army.

ROMAN WEAPONS
The rectangular shield (*scutum*) and heavy lance (*pilum*) became less common and were replaced by oval or round shields and lighter spears such as the *lancea*. Some units also carried up to five lead-weighted darts per man. The single volley of *pila* traditionally thrown in Roman battles just before combat was replaced by a much longer barrage of darts, javelins and arrows fired by archers in close support. Most units seem to have worn scale or mail armour and iron helmets if they were available. The quantity of heavily armoured horse did increase, especially in the Eastern army.

PRELUDE TO BATTLE
At Adrianople, the Gothic leaders Colias and Sueridus revolted and laid siege to the city. Besieging cities was not a Gothic strongpoint, and in time they stopped their siege and joined the wider revolt. The situation was precarious and the Roman commander Lupicinus requested help from Valens. Valens in turn asked for assistance from his nephew Gratian, emperor of the Western Roman Empire. Both emperors moved units towards the Goths. The Goths now had no choice but to continue the fight: they could not go home.

The Romans had been pursuing a defensive policy but when Valens arrived the tide turned. He drove the Goths from around Constantinople. It is reported that before his departure from Constantinople, Valens was distressed by a letter from Gratian informing him of victory over the Lentienses, a Germanic tribe. Valens did not want to be outshone by his nephew or his own commanders. He marched to Adrianople, where he left his imperial seal and field treasury for safekeeping.

Valens' scouts erroneously reported a force of 10,000 Goths in the area. At Adrianople Valens pitched camp to await Gratian's reinforcements and reinforced the city with defensive earthworks. The days were very hot and dusty. It was reported that Gratian was approaching. Valens was prepared to strike now, if he could find the enemy.

Fritigern sent envoys to the Romans to buy time, but the Romans refused to listen to their requests. Valens believed that in a few days, after he had beaten them in battle, he would not need to compromise. Fritigern also set fire to the surrounding fields, sending up huge clouds of smoke.

DEPLOYMENT OF TROOPS
On 9 August AD 378, a scorching sun was obscured by enormous clouds of smoke from the still burning fields. The Roman army marched out at dawn. It seems highly unlikely that Valens did not know the rough whereabouts of the Goth encampment. He ordered his army to march in a column of battle rather than the more usual defensive square. They unexpectedly came upon the Goth camp.

The Goths had made a huge, defensive, circular structure from the wagons on which they travelled with their families and possessions. Within this 'laager' of wagons was the main group of Goths. Both sides were

WHO WERE THE GOTHS?

The Goths (or, in Latin, *Getae*) came from the broad region we now call Germany, but their origins are not completely known. According to their own traditions they came from Scandinavia and emigrated through Poland and the Ukraine to the Black Sea region.

The Goths did not all live together in a country with borders and cities and towns, but rather as a number of self-contained units of population in the area spreading from the River Danube to the Crimean region on the northern shores of the Black Sea. The Goths had no government, nor any form of authority structure that created a central organization or administration. The self-contained units of people, or clans as we might call them, were led by charismatic warriors. These were strong men with military success behind them who grew in reputation and power and became leaders of their people by performing deeds that impressed them. Leadership of that kind, however, is fragile: it rests above all upon reputation, and so can be challenged and defeated at any time.

Among the many Goth clans were the Tervingi, who occupied the area north of the Danube, and the Greuthungi, who lived further east. Later they migrated further westward and came to be known as the Visigoths and Ostrogoths. According to Tacitus, the Goths were distinguished by their round shields, short swords and powerful loyalty towards their warrior chiefs.

As they spread through central Europe and down towards the Black Sea region in the third century AD, the Goths seem to have exerted a great deal of pressure on the indigenous tribes they encountered on the way, pushing them on to the borders of the Roman Empire and creating a lot of conflict with the Romans.

taken by surprise, an indication that neither side's intelligence was particularly effective. At 2 p.m., without having taken food or water that day, thousands of Roman soldiers stood in formation a few kilometres outside Adrianople. The Romans must have been not only hungry, but also exhausted. They had marched to the battlefield and had been in full armour under the blazing sun since dawn.

The Romans now attacked. Perhaps Valens still thought that the report of 10,000 Goths was true, which would explain why he engaged the enemy so quickly. It seems more likely, however, that he was motivated by jealousy of Gratian's successes rather than by sound military strategy.

THE COURSE OF THE BATTLE

The Romans advanced their infantry centre to meet the circle of Gothic wagons, weakening their rear as the line bent to bring the whole of the front line in contact with the Goths. The Roman cavalry on the left wing was still riding up to the battlefield and was not able to deploy effectively.

In the rush to assemble and charge, the Roman units on the left became separated. At that critical juncture, cavalry of the Greuthungi clan, who had been away from the camp finding grazing for their horses, came on the scene and attacked the Roman rear, at a vital point where the left wing of the cavalry linked up with the central columns of infantry. This only increased a problem common in infantry battles of the time. Infantry moves too far to the right, as each infantryman looks for protection from the shield carried by the comrade on his right. Modern historians argue that success of the non-Tervingi Goths at Adrianople lay in surprise and timing, rather than overwhelming numbers. Their mounts were among the few horses present among the Goths.

The Roman infantry lost control and became a confused mass. Great clouds of dust added to this confusion. Gothic archers surrounded them and cut them down. Valens attempted to rally his forces but he could not find his auxiliary reserve, the Batavi. Soon, thousands lay dead and dying, including Valens himself.

AFTERMATH

Ammianus tells us that scarcely one third of the Roman army escaped. The loss of so many commanders may have been a heavier blow than the loss of soldiers. Gratian was delayed by a further revolt among the Germanic Alamanni, and then by sickness, but he seems to have genuinely done everything in his power to come to the aid of his uncle.

Encouraged by their victory, the Goths moved on to Constantinople. They vainly attempted to storm the city, then resorted to pillaging the countryside around it for supplies and booty. They were trapped in Thrace, unable to secure a crossing to Asia.

The strength of the Roman Empire was still great, because it was based on the successful absorption of so many different peoples and the prosperity it brought to its provinces. After the battle the Romans reverted to low-level harassment of the Goths and succeeded in forcing a treaty in AD 382.

Some historians have claimed that mediaeval warfare began on the battlefield of Adrianople, with its supremacy of cavalry. Others believe that the truth is less simple and that Adrianople is not such a clear turning-point in military tactics.

Roman infantry tactics tended to become more defensive as the quality of their troops declined, which indeed happened in the later Empire. The Roman army of this period was less effective than the professional army of earlier times, but it still tended to win most of its battles. As in earlier periods, it was rare for the army to deploy in fewer than two lines.

The charge of barbarian infantry that usually began a battle was sometimes met at a halt, to retain good order in the Roman ranks, but more often good order was sacrificed to advancing at a run. The average unit in the later army may not have had the discipline to advance slowly and silently.

The smaller size of the units meant that, while each formed an effective part of a line, they had little experience of operating in mutual support, and lacked a command structure to facilitate the good use of reserves. At Adrianople one unit of Batavi (troops from the Low Countries) was placed in reserve but could not be found when it was needed. Historians have argued that cavalry was more important than infantry in later Roman armies. It is difficult to prove this point. Possibly there was a slight change in emphasis in battle tactics. The ideal was still a balance of cavalry and infantry, with the latter in the majority.

Emperors campaigned away from Rome for extended periods. For much of the later Empire, civil war was going on everywhere. The Roman army adapted to fighting against forces whose arms and tactics were identical to their own. It became important to mobilize greater numbers of troops. Overall numbers probably increased, but the size of individual units, especially the legion, dwindled. The Roman army in this period seems to have been geared for low-level warfare. Unlike their predecessors, they were reluctant to engage in open, pitched battles. It took at least a year to prepare for a major foreign expedition. The professional army did not possess the great reserves of manpower that the old citizen militia had offered, and it was harder to raise troops quickly. More and more officers and soldiers in the Roman army were 'barbarians', that is, non-Romans.

TROOPS AT ADRIANOPLE

ROMAN ARMY – TOTAL 21,000
Cataphracts – 500
Roman heavy cavalry – 3,000
Roman archers – 500
Roman Legions, heavy infantry – 8,000
Auxilia Palatina, heavy infantry – 9,000

THE GOTHS – TOTAL 24,500
Tervingi and Greuthungi heavy cavalry – 4,000
Tervingi heavy infantry – 18,000
Tervingi foot archers – 2,000
Alan and Hun warriors – light cavalry archers – 500

CHÂLONS AD 451

BACKGROUND

When the Huns first appeared on the edges of the Roman Empire, it seemed that they might present a serious threat to peace; but they settled down on the Great Hungarian Plain, in the flatlands around the Tisza and Danube rivers. For almost 50 years they served the Romans as allies more often than they attacked them as enemies. From the 420s onwards, however, the eastern emperor Theodosius II was forced to pay annual tribute to the Huns after he lost an entire army to them. The decisive turn in events was the accession of Attila as king of the Huns.

Attila was much more aggressive and ambitious than his predecessor and managed to unite the Huns. He led an invasion of southeastern Europe in AD 441, sacking cities in the Balkans, and also a march on Constantinople, forcing Theodosius to increase his payments. Yet in AD 450 he focused his ambitions on the west. The various forces of that region were in disarray and Attila hoped to play them off against each other. Valentinian III, the western Roman emperor, faced threats to his empire from Gaiseric, king of the Vandals, and Theodoric, king of the Visigoths. Yet Attila's principal opponent was the ambitious Roman general Aetius, who had campaigned in Gaul against various tribes for the past 30 years, and now effectively acted as monarch there.

In AD 450 the new emperor, Marcian, announced that he would no longer pay the annual tribute to Attila. Attila protested, demanding that the emperor's sister marry him and thus make him heir to the Western Roman Empire. He then prepared to cross the Rhine and attack the west. Both he and Aetius set about collecting allies. Attila tried to persuade the Visigoths to join his cause, but Aetius managed to recruit them instead, as well as the Alans and Sarmatians. Attila enlisted the support of the Germanic tribes, under their king Ardaric.

THE ROMAN EMPIRE IN THE FIFTH CENTURY AD

Apart from a brief period when it was reunited by the emperor Constantine in the middle of the fourth century, the Roman Empire had been split in two since AD 286. When Attila crossed the Rhine to attack the western Empire, he threatened a tottering relic of power which had already been ravaged by many barbarian tribes. The Visigoths had an independent kingdom in Aquitaine in Gaul, while Vandals occupied North Africa with a capital at Carthage. Roman rule hardly existed in many parts of Gaul and Spain.

HUN TACTICS

The Huns' tactics were intended to break the enemy up, luring small groups away so that they could be surrounded and overwhelmed. In a sense they acted rather as if they were hunting. They tended to avoid pitched battle and rely on surprise. The Hun tactics in battle were not, in fact, so very different from those practised by a wide range of those groups in northern Eurasia that deployed mounted bowmen as their main

THE ROMAN GENERAL AETIUS

In his youth, Aetius had lived among the Huns as a child hostage, so he knew a great deal about his enemy. By AD 451, aged 61, he had been the foremost general in the Roman Empire for many years, and the chief political adviser to the emperor Valentinian. The Empire in the west had suffered staggering setbacks throughout his lifetime, but Aetius had done more than anyone to keep what remained of the Roman world strong and prosperous. His achievements in building a coalition against the Huns should not be underestimated. Uniting Visigoths, Alans and Franks under one military banner with their traditional enemy, the Romans, for the defence of Gaul, was a remarkable feat.

THE ROMAN ARMY STRUCTURE IN THE FIFTH CENTURY AD

By the fifth century AD the western Roman army was in a decadent state. It relied enormously on foreign troops, and increasing numbers of officers and soldiers were 'barbarians'. The distinction between citizen and non-citizen troops had virtually disappeared. Aetius relied on hired foreign troops for all his campaigns in Gaul, and even before the battle of Châlons had occasionally used Huns.

The professional army did not possess the great reserves of manpower of the old citizen militia. With the Empire declining markedly during this period, the structures were no longer in place to support and maintain large armies. Indeed, the battle of Châlons marks the first appearance of the smaller armies typical of the mediaeval era. Contemporary sources report troop numbers in the hundreds of thousands on both sides at Châlons , but in fact even an estimate of 25,000 men in the Roman army may be too large. It was difficult to raise troops quickly, and consequently preparing for major campaigns was a lengthy business. Nevertheless, the army continued to be the

fighting force. The basic approach was to loose volley after volley of arrows at the enemy and then move in for the kill in hand-to-hand fighting. The strategic mobility and sheer ferocity of the Huns terrified their enemies. Furthermore, looking and fighting differently from other barbarians gave them a significant psychological advantage.

GERMANIC TACTICS

The tactics of the Germanic troops were typical of most of the barbarians of the era. They were infantry-based armies who charged at a run, shoulder to shoulder, in deep formation, relying largely on their size and physical strength to batter down the opposition. Their shields were as much thrusting weapons as defensive ones. Lacking armour, they were relatively quick and mobile. The Germanic cavalry and archers were less effective.

Empire's largest employer, and its organization still had an enormous impact on the economy.

ROMAN WEAPONS
The rectangular shields and heavy lances of the past became less common and were replaced by oval or round shields and lighter spears. Some units also carried up to five lead-weighted darts per man. Battles began with a barrage of darts, javelins and arrows fired by archers in close support. Most units seem to have worn scale or mail armour and iron helmets, if they were available. The quantity of heavily armoured cavalry did increase, especially in the eastern army.

ROMAN ALLIES
Jordanes, a Goth historian of the sixth century AD, records that Aetius' coalition included Visigoths, Alans, Sarmatians, Armoricans, Liticians, Burgundians, Saxons, Olibrones and other Gallic or German tribes. All of these peoples had at various times been either allies or enemies of Rome. The Visigoths and Alans, in particular, had fought against Aetius in the past. Hence, at Châlons, Aetius' army was very much a confederation. The tactics of his barbarian allies would for the most part have been similar to those of Attila's Germanic allies. The exceptions were the Alans and Sarmatians, whose battle tactics were more closely related to those of the Huns.

PRELUDE TO BATTLE

Early in AD 451, Attila and his army crossed the Rhine along a wide front. His far left flank advanced along the Moselle towards Metz, the centre towards Paris and then Orléans, while the right wing swung wide towards Arras. They devastated the countryside, sacking and burning every city they approached. Paris, however, was saved, according to legend, by the prayers of a young girl, now remembered as St Geneviève. In May, Attila began laying siege to Orléans, then ruled by Sangiban, king of the Alans.

On hearing this, Aetius marched to Orléans, successfully enlisting the Visigoths, after persuading their normally hostile king, Theodoric, that Attila was the greater enemy. They relieved the besieged city and enlisted Sangiban and the Alans, just as they seemed ready to defect to Attila. Unwilling to be trapped around the walls of Orléans, Attila abandoned the siege and retreated to the open Champagne district of France. Recalling his distant right and left wings to join the main body of his army, he left a rear guard of the Gepids, an East Germanic tribe, at the Seine to cover his withdrawal. However, Aetius destroyed it in a night attack in which all of the Gepids are reported to have been killed or wounded.

The position that Attila chose to confront Aetius was a broad plain with high ground to his right (the Roman left). The exact site of the battle is disputed, but contemporary sources describe the Catalunian Plain in such terms that it must lie somewhere in the Champagne region of France in a triangular area bounded by Troyes, Mery-sur-Seine and Arcis, with the nearest major town being Châlons-sur-Marne. The Hun leader faced his army north. He commanded the Huns, his best troops, in the centre and placed his Germanic allies on either side.

Aetius deliberately placed Sangiban in the centre with his Alans, so that his least reliable troops would face whatever attack Attila might launch there.

Sandwiching Sangiban between himself and Theodoric appeared the best way to control the suspect Alan loyalty. But, more importantly, this formation held out the prospect of Aetius' own Roman force on the left and the Visigoths on the right executing a double attack on the enemy flanks.

THE COURSE OF THE BATTLE

On the morning of the battle there was some fighting on the Hun right flank over possession of the ridge. The Romans gained this high ground, which brought an advantage for their planned flank attack. After this tactical loss, Attila rallied his troops and ordered his Huns to attack the Alans directly in front of them. The Alans yielded ground but nevertheless fought well, maintaining their formation and withdrawing only slowly and under intense pressure. When the Huns had made some progress, Attila wheeled them left to hit the Visigoths in the flank. The Visigoths, who had successfully beaten back Attila's Germanic allies on their flank, however, turned inwards to lead a counterattack against Attila's forces. In heavy fighting, the Visigoths lost their king Theodoric. However, the threat from the Romans on the high ground to Attila's right, although they had not made dramatic headway against his Germanic allies there, was sufficient to make him withdraw. His forces in the centre were now separated from his flanks and faced the possibility of being enveloped on both sides. He therefore ordered a withdrawal to his wagon-parked base camp, which he reached by nightfall after a battle that had lasted all afternoon. Once there, the Hun archers beat back any Roman assault as night fell.

AFTERMATH

At first light on the following day, both sides were able to view the carnage of the previous day's fighting. Contemporary sources claim that the casualties were between 165,000 and 300,000, but such figures are

No name from history represents savagery as vividly as that of Attila the Hun. As late as the 20th century, one of the most offensive names that could be found for the Germans in both World Wars was 'Huns'. As the greatest Hun leader, Attila is the archetypal sacker of cities and killer of defenceless children. In his own day he and his Huns were known as the 'Scourge of God', and the devastation they caused in Gaul before the battle of Châlons became a part of mediaeval folklore and tradition.

It was said that Attila claimed to own the very sword of Mars, the Roman god of war, and that other barbarian chiefs could not look him directly in the eyes without flinching. In his great book *The History of the Decline and Fall of the Roman Empire*, the 19th-century English historian Edward Gibbon offers a famous description, based on an ancient account, of the personality and appearance of the Hun.

'His features, according to the observation of a Gothic historian, bore the stamp of his national origin: a large head, a swarthy complexion, small, deep-seated eyes, a flat nose, a few hairs in the place of a beard, broad shoulders, and a short square body, of a nervous strength, though of a disproportioned form. The haughty step and demeanour of the king of the Huns expressed the consciousness of his superiority above the rest of mankind; and he had a custom of fiercely rolling his eyes, as if he wished to enjoy the terror which he inspired. . . . He delighted in war; but, after he had ascended the throne in a mature age, his head, rather than his hand, achieved the conquest of the North; and the fame of an adventurous soldier was usefully exchanged for that of a prudent and successful general.'

Legend has it that Attila was a dwarf. He was not, but he did have a dwarf at his court. He was about 45 at the time of invasion.

Nowadays, Attila is seen as less of a monster. Recent archaeology and an account by the Thracian writer Priscus, who spent time at Attila's court, suggest a more enlightened and attractive figure. He was clearly a ruthless warlord, but in other respects it is possible that he was a wise and tolerant man. He was capable of clemency, for he pardoned a would-be assassin hired by the chief eunuch of the eastern Roman emperor to eliminate him. Attila was more than a great commander. He was a complex character and a striking personality.

WEAPONS OF THE HUNS

Huns were expert archers, and their combination of archery and horsemanship was devastating. They used a peculiarly strong composite bow, that is, a bow made from more than one type of material, such as wood, sinew, and horn. These were precious objects, carefully manufactured by specially trained Hun craftsmen, and their use required great skill, so they were not used for common purposes such as hunting. War bows and hunting bows were as different from each other as modern rifles and shotguns. The composite bow was quite accurate up to 50 to 60 metres and its effective range would be as much as 160–175 metres. It is said by Ammianus that the Huns tipped their arrows with bone arrowheads, but this has never been proved.

The lasso was also a feared Hunnic weapon, which could ensnare an enemy very effectively, particularly if he was struggling with wounds. The Huns' swords were heavy cutting weapons; the more heavily armoured Huns also fought with thrusting lances. Armour and helmets were possibly the privilege of the few who were rich enough to afford them. The Huns also obtained weaponry by plundering the arms of their Roman victims, but unlike other bararian tribes they do not seem to have had Roman craftsmen to manufacture their weapons.

TROOPS AT CHÂLONS

THE HUNNIC/GERMANIC ARMY
– TOTAL 25,000

1,000 Hunnic nobles, mounted, a small proportion of them wearing armour and helmets and carrying long lances as well as bows. The dress of the nobles was much the same as that of the ordinary warriors: felt boots, baggy trousers and a long-sleeved tunic. They are described as shaven-headed and, most people assume, were of a Mongolian appearance.

15,000 Hunnic warriors, mounted, mostly with no armour or helmets. They used composite bows, backed by hand axes or swords. Many carried lassos with which to unseat their enemies.

3,000 Gepids and Germanic cavalry, armed with thrusting spears, javelins, and swords. Most of them wore helmets and mail armour and carried round shields.

10,000 Germanic infantry, armed with throwing spears and swords or hand-axes. All carried large round or slightly oval shields, but very few had helmets, and even fewer wore mail armour. They were dressed in tight-fitting trousers and long-sleeved tunics.

1,000 Germanic archers, armed with bows and hand weapons. They did not wear armour.

THE ROMAN/ALLIED ARMY
– TOTAL 25,000

4,000 Roman heavy cavalry, armed with throwing/thrusting spears, javelins and swords, wearing helmets and mail or scale armour, and carrying round shields.

8,000 Roman infantry, armed with throwing spears and swords, wearing helmets and armour and carrying large oval shields painted with symbols representing their units. Some men in the rear ranks may have had bows. The infantry were dressed in long-sleeved tunics and close-fitting trousers. Legions were much smaller in this period, numbering some 1,000 men, were no longer of quite such high quality and tended to operate in pairs.

6,000 Visigoth cavalry (including Franks and Saxons), armed with thrusting spears, javelins, and swords. Most of them wore helmets and mail armour and carried round shields.

8,000 Visigoth warriors (including Franks and Saxons), armed with throwing spears and swords or hand-axes. All carried large round or slightly oval shields, but very few had helmets, and even fewer wore mail armour. They were dressed in tight-fitting trousers and long-sleeved tunics.

1,000 Visigoth archers (including Franks and Saxons), armed with bows and hand weapons, but wearing no armour.

500 Alan/Sarmatian nobles, mounted, a small proportion wearing armour and helmets and bearing long lances as well as bows. They were dressed in felt boots, baggy trousers and long-sleeved tunics.

2,000 Alan/Sarmatian horse archers, most of whom had no armour or helmets. They used composite bows, backed up by hand-axes or swords. Many carried lassos with which to unseat enemies.

500 Alan/Sarmatian infantry, clothed like the cavalry but armed with two-handed axes.

enormously exaggerated. Still, the battle was clearly unusually bloody.

Rather than attack the strong Hun position, Aetius and Thorismund, the new king of the Visigoths, decided on a siege. There were occasional hints of a renewed attack from the Hun camp, but they were little more than psychological harassment; the Huns had lost a significant number of men, and Attila was not prepared to reopen the battle.

In the end, however, Aetius decided against an all-out siege. He urged Thorismund to return with his forces to Aquitaine and secure his position on the throne. Some historians, both ancient and modern, have speculated that Aetius wished to ensure the loyalty of the Visigoths by keeping the Huns as a threat. Doubtless the strong Visigoth performance in the battle would have been of some concern to the Romans, in that it could have encouraged Thorismund to believe that an alliance with the Romans was unnecessary.

Attila died two years later, after a night's drinking following another wedding. Before that, however, Aetius may have regretted his decision to let the Huns off the hook and retreat back over the Rhine. In AD 452 Attila crossed the Alps into Italy, where he sacked numerous cities and again threatened Rome. Tradition has it that he was dissuaded from attacking the city by the pope, Leo I, also known as Leo the Great. But with the death of its ruler the Hun empire collapsed.

Aetius' success against the Huns and his effective treatment of the Visigoths in Gaul rendered him too skilful to be allowed to live, and in AD 454 Valentinian killed him personally with the imperial sword. One of the emperor's advisers said, 'You have cut off your right hand with your left.' The following year, two of Aetius' followers retaliated by killing the emperor and, within a generation, by AD 476, there would no longer be a Roman emperor in the west. Aetius was truly 'the last of the Romans'.

The Romans' defeat of the Huns stopped the Asian spread westward, paving the way for the collapse of Attila's empire two years later. Yet some have seen this battle as a victory of 'civilized' Christians over 'barbaric' heathens. In the immediate aftermath, this confirmed Christian power in western Europe, but the myth that evolved around the battle later became central to Europe's cultural memory throughout the mediaeval era. With the gradual demonization of Attila and the building up of Aetius as 'the last of the Romans', the battle came to be viewed as a definitive triumph of good over evil. Such a myth conveniently ignores the fact that many of Aetius' allies at the battle were barbarian heathens themselves. Yet that in turn demonstrates that the battle was a uniquely 'international' conflict for that period of European history. Both armies consisted of combatants from many peoples and the battle's effect was felt widely.

WHO WERE THE HUNS?

The Huns emigrated from Asia, but their origins are impossible to define accurately. They were unable to expand into the more settled regions of China, and so migrated westwards over several centuries, spreading themselves over a vast area and fighting everyone they came in contact with. It was after they crossed the Don River, in what is now Russia, in AD 375 that they came to be called 'Huns'. Their arrival put pressure on the Alans, Goths and other eastern European tribes, forcing them to move east and west to avoid fighting them. Through the latter part of the fourth century and the first quarter of the fifth, the Huns conquered territory north of the Danube as far west as modern Germany, with occasional raids against the eastern Roman Empire's capital of Constantinople. They were initially nomadic horsemen, bound to one another by kinship ties, travelling in small bands to maximize grazing for their horses. It was only in the fifth century that they settled in a fixed place and recognized an official monarch over their population, King Rua.

Ammianus describes the Huns as follows: 'The nation of the Huns . . . surpasses all other barbarians in wildness of life . . . And though [the Huns] do just bear the likeness of men (of a very ugly pattern), they are so little advanced in civilization that they make no use of fire, nor any kind of relish, in the preparation of their food, but feed upon the roots which they find in the fields, and the half-raw flesh of any sort of animal. I say half-raw, because they give it a kind of cooking by placing it between their own thighs and the backs of their horses.'

He also describes them as having 'squat bodies, strong limbs and thick necks' and says that they were 'almost glued to their horses, which are hardy it is true, but ugly, and sometimes, they sit on them woman-fashion, and thus perform their ordinary tasks. And when deliberations are called for about weighty matters, they all consult for a common object in that fashion.'

The Huns' reputation for cruelty was not undeserved. In the 440s Attila attacked a city in the Danubian provinces of the Balkans. The Huns so devastated the place that, when Roman ambassadors passed through to meet with Attila several years later, they had to camp outside the city on the river, for the stench of death in the city was so great that no one could enter. The riverbanks were still strewn with human bones. Many cities of Gaul suffered the same fate.

LION tv time COMMANDERS SERIES

'SCORECARD' SUMMARY FOR PARTICIPANTS

BATTLE	PLAYERS	SIDE PLAYED	RESULT
Qadesh	Teacher/Students	HITTITES	Lost
Marathon	Ipswich Sailors	GREEKS	Lost
Leuctra	Netball Team	THEBANS	Won
Gaugamela	Childhood Friends	ALEXANDER	Won
Telamon	*Pilot* Magazine	GAULS	Lost
Trebia	Amateur Dramatics	CARTHAGINIANS	Lost
Raphia	Celebrities	EGYPTIANS	Won
Cannae	Bedfordshire Police	CARTHAGINIANS	Won
Silarus River	Bristol Ferryboat	SLAVES	Won
Tigranocerta	Music Teachers/Students	ARMENIANS	Won
Bibracte	London Headhunters	ROMANS/CAESAR	Won
Pharsalus	Nottingham Uni Graduates	POMPEY	Lost
Watling Street	Lyme Park National Trust	ROMANS	Lost
Mons Graupius	Rose Family	CALEDONII	Lost
Adrianople	Milton Keynes Counsill...	ROMANS	Lost
Abritus	Army Cadets	HUNS	Lost

LORD WANDSWORTH COLLEGE SCHOOL – TEACHER & STUDENTS

PETER BOOTH / From: Hook, Hampshire, on school campus / Age: 56 / Occupation: History Teacher

Peter has been a teacher for 31 years. He now teaches 11–17 year olds, mainly at LWC. His great-uncle was Lieutenant John Chard, VC, hero of the battle of Rourke's Drift, and another ancestor is Lieutenant John Yule, who was with Nelson when he died. Peter has also run the Old Boys/Girls Association for three years, which builds contacts with ex-pupils. The school's most famous ex-pupil is Johnny Wilkinson.

JAMES AUGUSTINE / From: Basingstoke, Hampshire (day boy) / Age: 16 / Occupation: Secondary School Student studying A Levels in Economics, History, Biology and Physics

James's proudest moment was flying solo after ten years, achieving silver flying wings status. He wants to join the RAF when he has finished his education, but if not he'll follow a medical career.

James is good at chess and checkers, has experience of strategy PC games, is a member of the combined cadet force at school and loves sports, particularly rugby, tennis, hockey and weight training. He plays in a rock band and has played guitar since he was twelve. He also plays violin and drums.

SAM BISHOP / From: Basingstoke, Hampshire / Age: 16 / Occupation: Secondary School Pupil studying AS Levels in History, Latin, Biology, Chemistry and History

Sam is the most competitive team member and is likely to get 'edgy and fractious' if all does not go well. He's also the most experienced strategist as he has played real-time strategy games, such as *Shogun*, as well as chess. Sam is going to study history at university, is a self-confessed 'not-sporty' person, yet likes cross-country running, cycling, swimming and fell walking in the lake district. He also has no idea how to make a cup of tea! A potential history professor, Sam was once a child model for Mothercare.

VICKY GILDAY / From: Hook, Hampshire / Age: 16 / Occupation: Secondary School Pupil studying A Levels in History, Latin, German and Music.
Vicky is the only girl of the group but is determined to get her own way. She plays many instruments, including flute (grade 8), piano (grade 6), and viola, as well as singing (grade 7) in various choirs and swing bands. She loves music, pop to Renaissance, and played lead in the school production of 'Grease'. Vicky will either study music or history at university and is also interested in Roman archaeology.

IPSWICH SAILORS

DAVE CHISHOLM (Chiz) – partner to Kerry / From: Ipswich / Age: 36 / Occupation: Managing Director of composites engineering firm (Sailing: Helmsman/ Tactician)
Dave has sailed at numerous National, European and World Championships and coaches young sailors in the Ipswich region. He was a member of the British Olympic Team at the Sydney Games as the transport and logistics manager for the entire team. He was in the navy for thirteen years as a helicopter engineer and represented the RN in the sailing team. He has competed in the Inter-Ship Field Gun Competition three times. He left the navy mainly because they wouldn't promote him, and partly for a bet!

KERRY RYAN (Kez, Kezzer) / From: Ipswich / Age: 22 / Occupation: Multi Media Technician (Sailing: Navigator and Trimmer)
Kerry sails 12- and 14-foot dinghies and has competed at several sailing championships, but is currently concentrating on the National 'Firefly' Class, with Dave (Fireflies, an old and simple design, are raced in many clubs all over the country. They are considered one of the hardest classes in sailing to succeed in). She wants to win the national championships one day. Kerry was a girl guide, so is used to military discipline, and practises karate, which gives her focus and makes her a good forward thinker.

ANDREW 'Drew Man' JAMES / From: London / Age: 42 / Occupation: Insurance Director (Sailing: Helmsman/Trimmer)
Andrew has done lots of big-boat racing and cruising, including a trans-Atlantic trip with only four people on board (usually there are eight to twelve). He sails dinghies for the fun of the big events and to keep his hand in. He plays guitar – most recently with Dave after a few pints, but played seriously in some half decent local bands for quite some time. He still has a great singing voice, as he proved recently at a friend's birthday bash!

SCOTT DAWSON (Scotty, Snotty) / From: Warsash, near Southampton / Age: 24 / Occupation: Composite Engineer (Sailing: Crewboss and Trimmer)
Scott has raced everything from 60-foot yachts to dinghies and is very determined to win. Sailing tests your ability as you fight the elements and other teams, and always have to out-think the enemy and conditions, so he is used to strategic planning. He has worked on lots of high-performance racing yachts organising up to twenty people. He doesn't like to lose – unless he can blame it on someone else! He plays lots of sports, including rugby and football, and also enjoys kite flying on the beach – and loves to scare little dogs and knock people over.

LADIES' NETBALL TEAM

KELLY WEST / From: East London / Age: 27 / Occupation: Manager of www.socialsports.co.uk
Kelly co-ordinates social netball leagues around London: everything from managing umpires to running the website. She is Australian and has travelled extensively in the Middle East, Turkey, Thailand, Cambodia and Lebanon. Kelly is also into yoga and touch football.

ANITA KELSEY / From: North West London / Age: 25 / Occupation: Job Manager, London Underground
Anita calls herself 'the mediator' and her nickname is 'Mute to Madness'. A Kiwi who has been in Britain for two and a half years, Anita loves to travel and experience different cultures. She deals with track maintenance at LU, is strong minded and bossy. She works with only men, so says she is used to being forceful to get her voice heard.

MAGS KING / From: South East London / Age: 26 / Occupation: Procurement Agent, London Underground
Mags negotiates tenders, contracts and money for LU. She recently completed a 60-mile cycle for charity and also dives and skateboards. Aggressive and organised, Mags is the netball team captain.

KIRSTEN BEACOCK / From: East London / Age: 28 / Occupation: Company Secretariat, London Underground
Kirsten works in the legal department of LU. She loves history, especially the Tudors and Stewarts, Henry VIII and the Wars of the Roses. She is also an avid netball and football player and is an ex-*Risk* player. Kirsten hates to lose.

CHILDHOOD FRIENDS

RICHARD SPENCER / From: London / Age: 38 / Occupation: Senior Business Strategy Manager for BT for 14 years
Richard's job is to understand his competitors' strengths and weaknesses and plan strategies to beat them, and to set prices. His dad was head of the Mediaeval Dept at the Museum of London, so hopefully he's picked up a few tips.

JON FOX / From: Sheffield / Age: 38 / Occupation: IT/Comms Manager, former Rat Catcher & Pest Controller
Jon has a degree in Crop Protection! All four convene annually to play games including *Dungeons & Dragons* and pretend to be thirteen years old again. He is soon to abseil off Sheffield United Football ground . . .

RICHARD MARSHALL / From: London / Age: 38 / Occupation: Freelance Photographer
Richard is the only one of the group who is not married with kiddies. He was originally on a science and engineering career path, but at 23 travelled the world and learned Spanish. He is now a bit of a hippy, a poet and folk guitarist.

NIGEL DAVIES / From: London / Age: 37 / Occupation: Eye Surgeon, so is a 'dab hand with a laser'
Nigel is the brightest member of the team – he has two degrees, one from Oxford, where he was captain of the fencing team. However, despite his degrees he has spent twenty years trying to build a synthesiser from a kit, which still doesn't work.

PILOT MAGAZINE

**NICK BLOOM / From: Hemel Hempstead / Age: 53 /
Occupation: Deputy Editor**

Nick is an aerobatics pilot, has been in a one-man band, flies his plane to work and has a great knowledge of history and battles. He is Europe's premier aerobatics pilot, an aviation romance author and once ran his own research company, mainly dealing in focus groups.

**DAVE CALDERWOOD / From: Shabbibgton, Bucks. / Age: 50 /
Occupation: Editor-in-Chief**

Dave is very professional – calm and relaxed under pressure, he never gets ruffled. He has been a journalist for thirty years and loves motorbikes. He has raced and tested them for fifteen years. Dave flies a four-seater plane. He used to own one, but says now his family takes all his cash.

**TRIX TRIANNI / From: Saffron Walden, Essex / Age: 32 /
Occupation: Art Editor**

Trix is glamorous and creative. She works for *Pilot* and *Sports Diver*, has fourteen years' experience designing magazines and lightens the team immensely. Her mum is Roman! She loves her job and is a good listener.

**DAVE FOSTER / From: Saffron Walden, Essex / Age: 25 /
Occupation: Advertisement Manager**

This Dave is the comedian of the team. He has tonnes of energy, can sell anything to anyone, is very competitive and doesn't want to be second best at anything. He loves people and sport, and is committed and passionate.

MACCLESFIELD AMATEUR DRAMATICS SOCIETY

SIMON WARING / Occupation: Senior Internal Sales Engineer

Simon is responsible for dealing with key accounts and providing technical and commercial advice on his company's products and services. He has been the membership secretary of Macclesfield Amateur Dramatics Society since 1991 and loves acting, outdoor activities of various kinds and playing drums and singing in a jazz band. His ambition is to sing with a big band, like Frank Sinatra.

ROB COPELAND / Occupation: Northern Sales Executive for a large fashion accessories firm based in London, selling ladies' handbags, purses and briefcases around the UK

Rob's father was an agent for the same company and, as a boy, Rob used to travel around with his dad, so he started very young. He plays the violin, but not very well, and enjoys going to antique auctions. He also collects miniature paintings from the nineteenth century. He started acting in 1998 with a small am dram group and joined MANS in 2000. Has done 22 productions in 4 years and loves being on stage. His ultimate ambition is to appear in a Shakespeare play in Stratford.

AIDAN JONES / Occupation: Clinical Data Associate (validates data collected for clinical trials)

Aidan joined MADS only six months ago and has played a butler and footman in *An Ideal Husband*. He studied Latin at school, which will help with the Romans! He's a big football fan and supports Wrexham, so is used to losing. He still harbours his childhood ambitions to win the FA Cup, and land on the moon! At school he attended extra classes on megalithic science (the study of stone circles and ley lines etc.). Other areas of historical interest are: the Napoleonic wars and fictional sea battles, particularly by Alexander Kent and Bernard Cornwell.

RANI JACKSON / Occupation: Schoolteacher

Rani played chess for England in her youth. She won the British Ladies Competition against Scotland and Wales, and played at the British Chess Championships every year for about ten years. She joined MADS in 1998 and always plays the foxy chicks and *femmes fatales*.

CELEBRITIES

RAJI JAMES / Acted in *EastEnders* – previously in *The Bill* and *East Is East*

An avid *Risk* player, Raji also loves 3D battle re-enactments, especially *Braveheart*. His kids will be watching, so he has to win. Raji's former jobs include cab driver, barman, sandwich delivery man and foreman on a building site.

RICKY GROVES / *EastEnders*

Ricky used to be a chef and is still a keen cook. He also enjoys golf and fishing. His comedy heroes are Phil Cool and Tommy Cooper and he used to love *Doctor Who*, 'for the monsters'. Ricky's character in *EastEnders* is married to a Slater sister (Lynne), so he'll be used to living in a war zone.

KATE SILVERTON / BBC political programme *Weekend* with Rod Liddle

Kate has lived on a kibbutz in Israel, travelled with the Bedouins in Egypt and helped build a school and bridges in Zimbabwe. She was a national swimming champion and has a degree in psychology and also read business management and Arabic. She worked in the City as a corporate financier before joining the BBC as a journalist.

AL MURRAY / Comedian

Murray's grandfather, Sir Ralph Murray, was a diplomat and possibly a spy, heading the so-called Information Research Department set up to discredit Russia. And his great-great-great-great-grandfather was William Makepeace Thackeray. Al read modern history at St Edmund Hall, Oxford, and reads everything there is to read about wars.

BEDFORDSHIRE POLICE

**SARAH WILKINSON / From: Bedford / Age: 32 /
Occupation: Media Officer**

Sarah's job is to give information to the media about incidents ranging from missing dogs to murders, through interviews, briefings and promotions. She used to be a journalist and fell into this job by accident. She is a self-confessed history nut – she did a History degree, watches every history documentary she can and reads loads of history books. Her greatest love is football. She owns shares in Norwich City (her home town) and her adopted team, Bedford Town, and is known for feisty renditions of club songs.

STEVE DILLEY / From: Bedford / Age: 45 / Occupation: Superintendent

Steve now divides his time between working in HR – training, recruiting and staff development – and his operational role. He's been in the police for 23 years and before that he was a trombone player in the Guards. He admits to being competitive and is a commander and tactical advisor for public disorder. In contrast to his job, he is a keen outdoors person, taking part in voluntary countryside maintenance, including laying hedges.

CLIFF DIXON / From: Bedfordshire / Age: 50 / Occupation: Deputy Chief Constable

Cliff's job involves responsibility for all operational policing and performance within Bedfordshire, including serious crime and major incidents. Before he joined the police he wanted to become a rock star or an artist. He now plays guitar and sings in a band (with Clare) and does a mean cover of 'Angels' by Robbie Williams. He says he can think logically in the most challenging situations, and be ruthless when necessary.

CLARE SIMON / From: Bedford / Age: 38 / Occupation: Police Superintendent

Clare is responsible for operational policing in North Bedfordshire, and over 250 staff. She is a Firearms Incident Commander, Public Order Commander and Trained Negotiator. She's climbed the 3 highest peaks in the UK in 36 hours and survived 2 divorces, but says her greatest achievement was trekking to Everest Base Camp. She plays the trumpet and is lead vocalist in a band called Bladerunner, who gig at pubs and social events. She also plays the cornet for Bedford Town Brass Band and appeared at the Royal Albert Hall in the national finals in 2000.

BRISTOL FERRYBOAT TEAM

ROB SALVIDGE / From: Bristol / Age: 45 / Occupation: Director/Skipper/Maintenance Manager

There are fifteen miles of waterway and river, for both ferrying work and for putting on trips. The company has 6 boats and employs 30–35 people, 10 of whom are full-time. Rob is married to the general manager of FBC, skippers passenger boats around Bristol harbour and fixes lots of things. He read *Biggles* books as a kiddie, read a bit about Nelson and has an interest in strategy. He loves sailing on big boats in the sunshine and has done ocean racing before.

ELISE HURCOMBE / From: Bristol / Age: 23 / Occupation: Marketing and Promotions/Education/Website

Elise is a commercial photographer/artist who also does private commissions, such as sound installations and sculpture. She also works with children in schools doing art workshops. Elise has been with FBC for four years. She started out as crew, then created her current job as promotions person for the company. She has been researching the history of Bristol Harbour for a new kind of computerised tour-guiding system.

BIDDY DYMOND / From: Bristol / Age : 33 / Occupation: Skipper/Runs office (summers only)

Because not very many women drive the boats, Biddy is very proud of getting her license. She confesses to being bossy, *very* competitive and a little confrontational, so she will get upset if her team starts to lose. She has worked on yachts in the Mediterranean, is also a cook, has done landscape gardening, is a massage therapist and has run restaurants. Last winter she went to Australia, Hong Kong and New York: she doesn't do winters in Britain!

DEAN WELLS / From: Bristol / Age: 33 / Occupation: Studying Music Technology at Bristol College, and crew on the ferries

Dean is the strategist of the team. He is involved in music production, DJ-ing on a Bristol local pirate radio station and various clubs in Bristol, and has done a great deal of travelling in Asia, South America and Europe. Dean has also meditated for two weeks with Tibetan monks and is therefore calm and chilled. He swam with alligators in the Amazon and was saved by pink dolphins.

MUSIC TEACHERS – DURHAM

EMMA FISK / Age: 30 / Occupation: Musician and Music Lecturer

Emma is a part-time lecturer in music in the Performing Arts department at EDHC College, an FE college in East Durham. She teaches music theory, aural awareness, performance skills and technology to BTEC Pop Music students, including Mark. She joined a rock band at the age of sixteen and spent the next seven years touring Britain and Europe in the obligatory white transit van. As a musician she performs regularly and is also currently completing a Masters degree in music at Newcastle University, specialising in studio composition and performance.

BILLY NICHOLSON / Age: 36 / Occupation: Music Lecturer and Songwriter

Billy teaches students about composition, performance and music technology. He was in a band full-time and was doing lots of gigs in Germany. Then the exchange rate changed and the band went into debt, so he started doing any kind of music work, including writing adverts, musicals and contemporary dance stuff and the odd bit of teaching here and there. He's currently in a band with Emma – his girlfriend – and is also learning the piano.

LEANNE TURTON / Age: 18 / Occupation: student

Leanne is into acting and singing, and is taking a Performing Arts course at college. She recently played the part of Countess Vigo, the bisexual arch villainess who sets out to reshape the world in her image with mind-altering drugs concealed in 'Exotic Love' beauty products. After leaving college, she hopes to make her dream of becoming an actress a reality. Her hobbies include creative writing, especially poetry, and socialising with her friends.

MARK BROADBENT / Age: 17 / Occupation: student

Mark loves music, has played the guitar for two years and is learning to play the piano. He is the lead singer in a band for which he writes original songs, and plays gigs in the north east area. He also enjoys drama and is a member of Centre Stage North-east and has played parts in many shows at Sunderland Empire Theatre. He attends East Durham & Houghall Community studying A-Levels in Performing Arts and Media, as well as a BND in Popular Music.

HEADHUNTERS

SIMON GOLDSWORTHY / From: London / Age: 30 / Occupation: Headhunter

Simon has a degree in History and worked as a historical tour guide for a year after graduating. He says he is an adrenaline junkie – he's a qualified ski instructor and divemaster, has a skydiving license and has run the London marathon. Like Ben, he's leaving headhunting soon to become a professional sailor. He reckons there will be a certain amount of good-humoured debate within their team, and if he feels knowledgeable he will lead.

DAVID HURWOOD / From: London / Age: 34 / Occupation: Headhunter
Until recently, Dave's landlord was Ben, so they worked and lived together. They get on well, apart from when Ben was pinching Dave's girlfriends. Dave says he is a natural leader, like all his team, and a proven coach at his workplace and for team sports. He plays rugby and football, waterskis, snowboards, is a qualified diver and says he is a better cook than Jamie Oliver! His ambition is to complete the Paris to Dakar race.

BEN O'REILLY / From: London / Age: 28 / Occupation: Headhunter
Ben has just handed in his notice to Steve as he's leaving City life to return to being a professional sailor. He hopes to be based in the Mediterranean in the summer and the Caribbean in the winter. His greatest achievement so far is crossing the Atlantic with a severe back injury, and his ambition is to cross the Pacific Ocean. He has a degree in PR and used to run a ski company. He says that his team mates are the most competitive individuals you could meet.

STEPHEN MCCARTY / From: London / Age: 34 /
Occupation: MD of his own headhunting company
Steve is his team mates' boss. He has started three recruitment businesses from scratch and says he always leads – his industry environment is high pressure and he thrives on it. He admits he can be devious and thinks many steps ahead. He has completed three marathons, one without any training, and his ambition is to cage dive with sharks in South Africa. He took a year out to write a novel, which is nearly finished – it features people who have annoyed him in real life being murdered.

NOTTINGHAM UNIVERSITY GRADUATES

BECKY ANSELL / From: Worcestershire / Age: 21 /
Occupation: Recent Graduate
Becky's teammate Tristan is also her boyfriend. They've been going out for two years and don't usually argue, although she thinks that *Time Commanders* may test their relationship! She wants to pursue a career in financial PR and eventually run her own company. Her main hobby is horse riding. She used to compete in horse trials all over the country until she went to university and couldn't devote enough time to it.

TRISTAN COWELL / From: Sheffield / Age: 22 /
Occupation: Graduate (taking year out)
Tristan is going out with Becky and he reckons she'll ignore all his advice as she normally does! Apparently she then comes back a while later and pretends it was all her idea. He is in the process of setting up his own company – he says he's 'exploring a few entrepreneurial avenues' – and his ambition is to earn lots of money for doing not much work. During his gap year before university he spent three months in Belize, central America, doing charity work, including building a school.

OLLY MENNELL / From: Harrogate / Age: 22 / Occupation:
Recent Graduate (starts job as a Venture Capitalist in September)
Olly has fulfilled his ambition to get a job as a venture capitalist and

wants to make his first million by the age of 26. He thinks that his study of strategy, and three years spent in the Officer Training Corps, will help him do well on *Time Commanders*. He says he only leads and is convinced that boys are better strategic planners than girls, a belief not shared by the girls on his team.

RUTH WILSON / From: Middlesex / Age: 21 /
Occupation: Recent Graduate
Ruth has just completed her degree in history and is going on to study drama at college in September. She says theatre is her passion and she loves being a drama queen – her ambition is to be a successful actress. She has directed one play and produced another play at the Edinburgh Festival. She says that she and Olly will probably argue over who is in charge of the team.

LYME PARK – NATIONAL TRUST PROPERTY

GARY RAINFORD / Age: 48 / Occupation: Head Gardener
Gary would love to take on a new National Trust garden that needs completely renovating. He loves his job – not only is it creative, but he's also creating something that will outlive him. He loves sci-fi and fantasy novels, is good at rifle shooting and archery and was in a Liverpool athletics club when he was younger. He plays lots of board games and computer games with his daughter.

PAUL MANSELL / Age: 52 / Occupation: National Trust Shop Manager
At the age of 22, Paul won a competition for Choreographer of the Year in the UK, beating 10 other choreographers (he is a trained modern dance teacher). He still does choreography in Sheffield for amateur groups and his ambitions are to appear in a West-end musical or to go on a major archaeological dig. He loves anything Celtic, and Kate Bush.

JO WRIGHT / Age: 28 / Occupation: Learning Officer
Jo is part of the education team, which includes the history of the National Trust estate. She wanted to be a primary school teacher, but escaped for a quieter, less stressful life. She wants to learn to play the piano, live in a hot country and have Jamie Oliver cook a meal for her and her friends. She enjoys Latin dancing, amateur dramatics and is currently learning how to water-ski.

GILL POMEROY / Age: 24 / Occupation: Visitor Service Assistant
Gill is very proud of the fact that she went snowboarding on her 21st birthday and managed to stay upright for more than five minutes. Her ambition is to live in a French vineyard and read lots of novels. Studied History for her first degree, does lots of drawing and painting and makes her own jewellery.

THE ROSE FAMILY FROM EDINBURGH

JO ROSE (daughter) / Age: 21 / Occupation: recently graduated from
a degree in Contemporary Theatre Practice at the RSAMD in Glasgow,
'so I guess that makes me . . . unemployed'
Jo has a pretty good understanding of the relevance of live art in contemporary culture and the ability to talk her way out of (or into) almost anything. She wants to become a 'C' list celeb, so she can do pantomime for the rest of her life. Alternatively she would like to be a tree, though is willing to start as a sapling, for the sake of the urban environment.

CAMERON ROSE (father) / Age: 49 / Occupation: Police Inspector
Cameron rules with a rod of iron that would give Hitler a run for his money. He is aiming to climb fifty Munros in the year leading up to his fiftieth birthday; so far he has done 34. He loves politics and history and his main interest is focused on the sixth century AD, which featured the Celtic saints. He is involved in many local committees, the local church and getting his letters published in *The Times*. He also looks after the church website.

SUE ROSE (mother) / Age: 47 / Occupation: Mother / Retired classroom assistant
Sue possesses an icy-cool diplomacy matched only by a rapier-sharp wit, fit to burst any bubble. She has an MA and a Secretarial Diploma and worked for five years in her local primary school as a special needs/classroom assistant. She now does three hours a month playing the piano for them. She loves being out in the wilds of Scotland – preferably by the sea or a river – and likes 'creating' things, such as jam and greetings cards, home-baking and DIY.

BEN ROSE (son) / Age: 19 / Occupation: Student (Politics and History at Strathclyde University)
Ben has had plenty of practice on computer games such as *Civilization*, *Championship Manager* and *Theme Hospital*. He used to draw up battle plans of Culloden or Bannockburn when he was young, to see how the experts did it. He loves football – he supports Aberdeen FC – and in 1993 won the Meadows Festival Cup for primary school football. He has just spent two weeks in Peru with a team helping with building work for a project for street children, and another fortnight assisting co-ordinating Overseas Student Welcome in Glasgow.

MILTON KEYNES COUNCILLORS

CLIVE CARRUTHERS / From: Milton Keynes / Age: 48 / Occupation: Councillor (Lib Dem) & Business Support Analyst
Clive was once a radio officer in the Merchant Navy, where he served in the North Sea on exploration oilrigs. He then became a coastguard officer, stationed in the Shetlands, so that he could spend more time on land with his two daughters. He has completed the Three Peaks Challenge twice for charity and cycled from John O'Groats to Lands End. He hopes to do the Inca Trail or cycle to China next year if he can get sponsorship. Clive also did two seasons as a Butlins Redcoat in the 70s.

ROBERT 'REX' EXON / From: Milton Keynes / Age: 39 / Occupation: Councillor (Lib Dem) & Supply Chain Management, ASDA
Rex's job involves trying to prevent ASDA's products from being sent to the wrong stores. He is a member of the Chartered Institute of Purchase and Supply and says he hates waste of any kind. He joined the Scouts as a boy and has been a Scout Leader for fifteen years. He's represented Britain at a World Jamboree and organised Jamborees in Thailand, Australia and Chile. He is also a climbing, abseiling and mountaineering instructor.

JAN LLOYD / From: Milton Keynes / Age: 59 / Occupation: Councillor (Labour) & Head Teacher
Jan has just retired as Head Teacher of a day and residential school for special needs pupils, having been a Head Teacher for over twenty years. In her political life she has spent many years as the Chair of the Strategic Committee. She thinks that will also help her perform well on *Time Commanders*. Her interests have included playing in orchestras, singing in choirs, including an opera group, riding and membership of Yorkshire County Cricket club for almost thirty years.

MARTIN CLARKE / From: Milton Keynes / Age: 47 / Occupation: Former Milton Keynes Councillor (Lib Dem), Parish Councillor & Company Director
Martin's company trains doctors, pharmacists and nurses within the NHS in management skills, helping them to think more strategically. He is writing a book on the subject. He is a keen volleyball player and is currently learning to sing. He says that councillors are often put under pressure in a public situation and have to react quickly, which is relevant to their task on *Time Commanders*. He also says they may decide to divide along party lines and fall out.

BRISTOL ARMY CADETS

GARY FORDER / From: Bristol / Age: 44 / Occupation: Cadet Admin Officer with Bristol ACF
Gary served in the army for 23 years and has been at ACF for nearly five years. He's a keen sportsman and lives to play football. He supports Bristol Rovers and is very proud of the fact. He eats for England and loves his butties. He also loves running and has run a fair few marathons in a charity style, and is going to run the Great Wall of China and attempt the Sahara Desert marathon.

IAN FISK / From: Trowbridge / Age: 51 / Occupation: Cadet Executive Officer with Bristol ACF
Ian is the boss, but rules with a fair hand. He encourages the group to work as a team and to be good problem solvers. An ex-Royal Marine Officer, he served all over the world, but gave it up to spend more time with his family – he's been married for 32 years. He has been with ACF for five years, and is the worst golfer he knows.

PAT MCSHERRY / From: Bristol / Age: 49 / Occupation: Cadet Admin Assistant
Pat, a Scotsman and ex-Royal Artillery warrant officer, joined the Army in 1972. Once a heavy smoker and drinker, he now runs half marathons and has become a svelte version of his former self. He loves golf, and his ambition is to beat Ian one day.

CHRIS STARBUCK / From: Bristol / Age: 42 / Occupation: Quartermaster
An ex-Army Officer, Chris is the person who gets all the equipment and counts it i.e. forks, spoons, clothing, bullets and bombs. He has been with ACF for two and a half years. He grew up in the Army, and attended about thirteen different schools. He has lived in the UK, Germany, Cyprus, Ireland and Hong Kong, where he was born. He loves motor biking around the country, and is also a runner – and has some national records in Hong Kong, including the 10,000 metres and steeplechase.

websites

This is a selection of websites that provide information on ancient history, general military history, Roman military history and Greek military history, and of sites where it is possible to read texts from classical historians in English.

GENERAL WEBSITES ON ANCIENT HISTORY

www.roman-emperors.org
De Imperatoribus Romanis: An Online Encyclopedia of Roman Emperors. An online encyclopedia of the rulers of the Roman empire from Augustus (27 BC–AD 14) to Constantine XI Palaeologus (AD 1449–1453). The encyclopedia includes an index of emperors; biographical essays on individual emperors; family trees of imperial dynasties, an index of significant battles; descriptions and maps of battles; maps of the empire at different times, and links to coin catalogues.

www.ukans.edu/history/index/europe/ancient_rome/
E/Roman/home.html
Lacus Curtius: a gateway to ancient Rome. An excellent general site that covers many aspects of the Roman world, with a Gazetteer locating where Roman towns and cities were, the texts of 19 complete works of Roman antiquity, a topographical dictionary of ancient Rome, sections on Roman Britain and the Later Empire, a Roman atlas and many subsites.

www.forumromanum.org
Forum Romanum provides a good deal of Rome-related material, with an entire section devoted to Latin texts, as well as sections on The Private Life of the Romans, Outlines of Roman History, Latin Language Resources and a Genealogy of the Gods.

www.livius.org
Livius is a wide-ranging site with material on many aspects of ancient history, including the history of ancient Greece, Rome, Persia, Germania Inferior, Judaea, Mesopotamia, Anatolia, Carthage and Egypt. It also has a picture archive.

www.roman-empire.net
Another site with plentiful material on ancient Rome, divided into the following sections: The Founding; The Kings; Early Republic; Late Republic; Early Emperors; The High Point; The Decline; The Collapse; Constantinople; Religion; Society; The Army, and a special Kids' Section. You can also create your own cutout Roman helmet to wear.

www.historyforkids.org
This site is designed to help children discover the history of many different parts of the ancient world, including Greece, Rome, India, Africa, Egypt, China and others. The site includes timelines and maps.

www.wsu.edu:8080/~dee/GREECE/GREECE.HTM
A comprehensive source on Greek history and philosophy.

www.perseus.tufts.edu/cache/perscoll_Greco-Roman.html#secondary1
Includes an excellent overview of ancient Greek history.

GENERAL WEBSITES ON MILITARY HISTORY

www.TheHistoryNet.com
A good general source for military history topics.

www.pvv.ntnu.no/~madsb/home/war/
A general site that includes the text of Sun Tzu's
Art of War.

www.militaryhistoryonline.com
A good general resource for military history
of all periods

ROMAN MILITARY HISTORY

www.barca.fsnet.co.uk
This is an excellent resource for everything about
Hannibal.

www.heraklia.fws1.com
A site that deals exclusively with Julius Caesar:
his life, exploits and death.

www.romanarmy.com
A comprehensive site for much to do with the Roman
army, including an encyclopedia and glossary
organized alphabetically by topic, an imagebase of
Roman military gravestones and a bibliography of
Roman military references.

www.romans-in-britain.org.uk
A comprehensive, clearly written site on everything to
do with Roman Britain, including: Britain before the
Romans; The Roman Expeditions; The Roman
Invasion; The Roman occupation; Decline of Roman
Britain; After the Romans departed; Britain and the
Romans; Roman architecture; Roman innovations;
The Romans at work; The Romans at leisure; Roman
military; Roman attractions in Britain.

http://myron.sjsu.edu
An excellent site with pages on Roman military history,
re-enactments, Roman women and other topics.

GREEK MILITARY HISTORY

dir.yahoo.com/Arts/Humanities/History/By_Time_
Period/Ancient_History/Greek/Military_History/
Good listing of different sites relevant to ancient
Greek military history.

www.ancientgreece.com/wars/wars.htm
Comprehensive list of links on ancient Greek wars.

www.teacheroz.com/greeks.html
This site has a huge listing of links on everything
to do with ancient Greece, with good links to general
and specific sites on wars in ancient Greece.

SOURCES

www.fordham.edu/halsall/ancient/asbook09.html
An excellent site for original sources on all aspects
of Roman and Greek antiquity. Allows the reader to
access many texts by the writers to whom we are
indebted for our knowledge of the ancient world,
including Xenophon, Herodotus, Caesar, Tacitus,
Plutarch and many others.

www.perseus.tufts.edu/cache/perscoll_Greco-
Roman.html
This is another very useful site for source material
by ancient Greek and Roman writers.

www.e-classics.com
This site contains compilations of texts by classical
authors, for example, '15 Ancient Greek Heroes'
from Plutarch's *Lives*.

BIBLIOGRAPHY

Adcock, F.E., The Greek and Maccdonian art of war (Berkeley 1957).

Allen, S., Celtic Warrior 300 BC–AD 100 (Oxford, 2001)

Anglim, S. et al, Fighting Techniques of the Ancient World (London, 2002)

Bradley, K.R., Slavery and rebellion in the Roman world (London 1989).

Caesar, The Gallic War (Oxford 1998).

Campbell, B., The Roman army 31 BC–AD 337: a source book (London 1994).

Caven, B., The Punic wars (London 1980).

Cheesman, G.L., The auxilia of the Roman imperial army (Oxford 1914).

Connolly, P., Greece and Rome at war (London 1981).

Daly, G., Cannae. The experience of battle in the second Punic war (London 2002).

Dawson, D., The origins of Western warfare. Militarism and morality in the Ancient World (Oxford 1996).

Delbrück, H., History of the art of war, volume I: warfare in antiquity (Lincoln and London 1990)

Delbrück, H., History of the art of war, volume II: the barbarian invasions (London 1990).

Ellis, J., Cavalry: The History of Mounted Warfare (New York 1978).

Elton, H., Warfare in Roman Europe AD 350–425 (Oxford 1996).

Evans, R.F., Legions of imperial Rome. An informal order of battle study (New York 1982).

Ferrill, A., The fall of the Roman Empire: the military explanation (London 1986).

Ferris, I.M., Enemies of Rome. Barbarians through Roman eyes (Stroud 2000).

Fields, N., Hadrian's Wall AD 122-410 (London 2003).

Gilliver, K. Caesar's Gallic Wars 58–50 BC (Oxford, 2002)

Goldsworthy, A., Cannae (London 2001).

Goldsworthy, A., The Punic Wars (London 2000).

Goldsworthy, A., Roman Warfare (London 2000).

Hackett, J. (ed.), Warfare in the ancient world (London 1989).

Hanson, V.D., 'From phalanx to legion 350–250 BC' in: G. Parker (ed.), The Cambridge illustrated history of warfare. The triumph of the West (Cambridge 1995).

Hanson, V.D., The Wars of the Ancient Greeks (London 1999).

Healy, M., Qadesh: 1300 (Oxford 1993).

Herodotus, The Histories (London 2003).

Keppie, L., The making of the Roman army from republic to empire (2nd edition) (London 1998).

Lazenby, J., Hannibal's war (Warminster 1978).

Lazenhy, J., The first Punic war (London 1996).

MacDonald, F., A Roman fort (Hove 1993).

MacDowall, S., Adrianople AD 378 (Oxford 1994).

MacDowall, S., Late Roman Cavalryman (London 1995).

Manley, J., AD 43 the Roman invasion of Britain. A reassessment (Stroud 2002).

Marsden, E.W., Greek and Roman artillery: historical development (Oxford 1999).

Nicolle, D., Atilla and the Nomad Hordes (Oxford, 1990)

Nicolle, D., Romano-Byzantine Armies (Oxford, 1992)

Parker, H.M.D., The Roman legions (rev. ed.) (Cambridge 1958).

Peddie, J., Hannibal's war (Stroud 1997).

Peterson, D., Roman legions recreated in colour photographs (London 1992).

Plutarch, Lives (London 1989).

Rich, J. and G. Shipley (ed.), War and society in the Roman World (London 1993).

Robinson, H.R., The armour of imperial Rome (London 1975).

Sadler, D., Scottish Battles (Edinburgh, 1996)

Sekunda, N., Marathon 490 BC (Oxford, 2002)

Sekunda, N., The Persian Army 560–330 BC (Oxford, 1992)

Sekunda, N., The Spartan Army (Oxford, 1998)

Shirley, E., Building a Roman legionary fortress (Stroud 2001).

De Souza, P., The Greek and Persian Wars 499–386 BC (Oxford, 2003)

Sumner, G., Roman army. Wars of the empire (London 1997).

Tacitus, Annals (London 1971).

Tacitus, The Agricola and the Germania (London 1970).

Warry, J.G., Warfare in the Classical World (Norman 1995).

Whitby, M., Rome at war AD 293–696 (London 2002).

Xenophon, Hellenica Books 5–7 (London 1989).

INDEX